ORBIS PICTUS
The Natural World

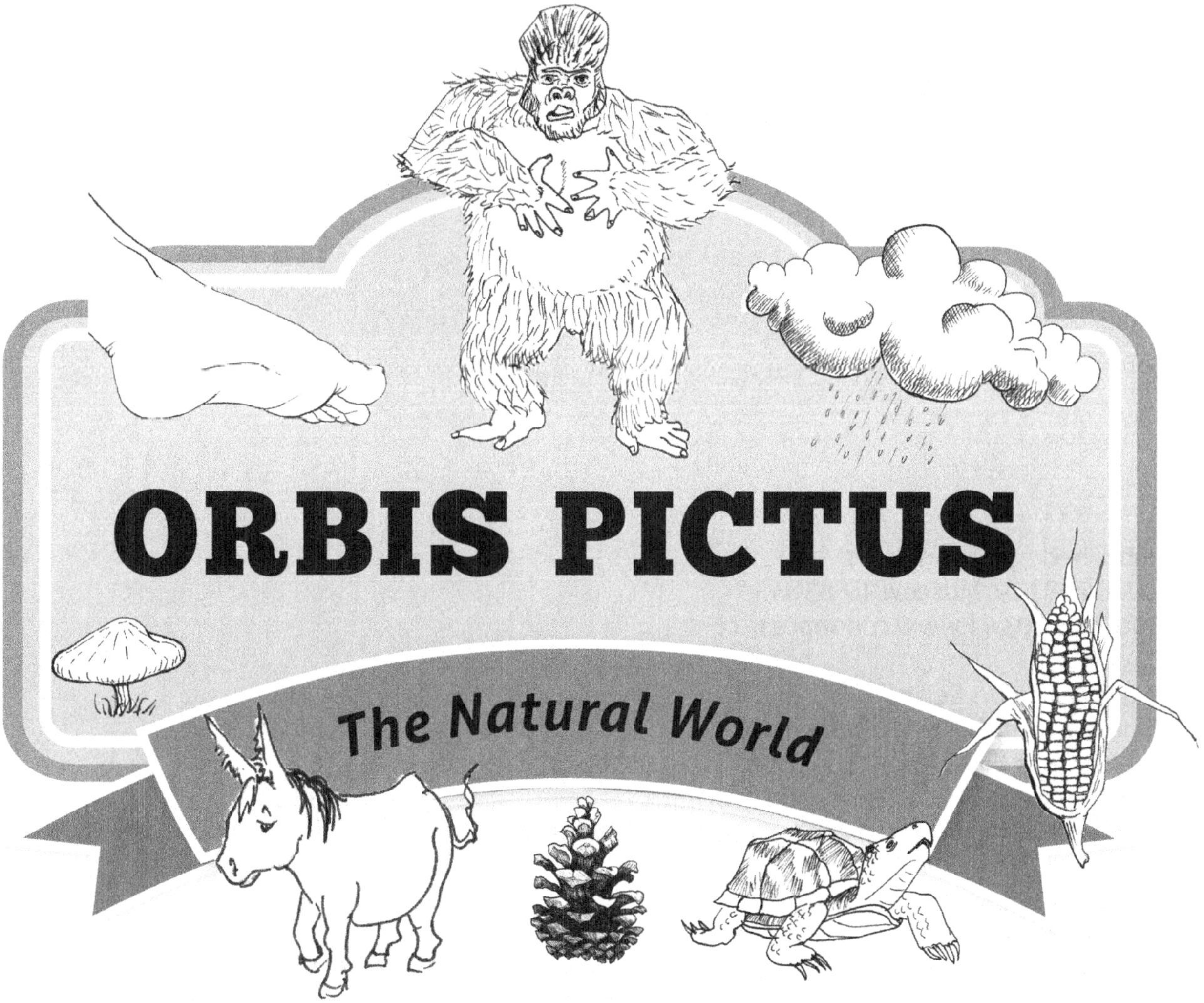

ORBIS PICTUS

The Natural World

Timothy Griffith

illustrations by Nathan Stevenson,
Sarah Schoolland, and Jessica Evans

Published by Canon Press
P.O. Box 8729, Moscow, ID 83843
800.488.2034 | www.canonpress.com

The *Orbis Pictus* Series
Timothy Griffith, *The Natural World*
Illustrations by Nathan Stevenson, Sarah Schoolland, and Jessica Evans
Text copyright © 2012 by Timothy Griffith
Illustrations copyright © 2012 by Nathan Stevenson, Sarah Schoolland, and Jessica Evans

Cover design by Rachel Rosales
Interior design by Laura Storm
Printed in the United States of America

All rights reserved. No part of this publication may be reproduced, stored in a retrieval system, or transmitted in any form by any means, electronic, mechanical, photocopy, recording, or otherwise, without prior permission of the author, except as provided by USA copyright law.

Library of Congress Cataloging-in-Publication Data

Griffith, Timothy.
 The Natural World / Timothy Griffith ; illustrations by Nathan Stevenson, Sarah Schoolland, and Jessica Evans.
    pages. cm. -- (Orbis pictus ; book 1)
 Summary: "Covers almost 500 words on the natural world. This includes not only words that appear frequently in Latin literature, but also those that have been adopted as technical terms in various scientific disciplines (especially biology)"--Publisher's blurb.
 ISBN 978-1-59128-116-0
 1. Latin language--Vocabulary--Juvenile literature. I. Title. II. Series: Orbis pictus (Moscow, Idaho) ; book 1.
 PA2387.G75 2012
 478.2'421--dc23
                                                        2012010336

13 14 15 16 17 18   9 8 7 6 5 4 3 2

CONTENTS

Introduction 7

1. Genera Animalium 12
2. Membra Quadrupedis 14
3. Membra Piscis et Avis 16
4. Bestiae Mansuetae 18
5. Bestiae Ferae 20
6. Magnae Bestiae 22
7. Parva Animalia 24
8. Aves Ferae 26
9. Aves Aquatiles 28
10. Aves Aliae 30
11. Bestiae Marinae 32
12. Bestiolae 34
13. Apes 36
14. Quae Gignuntur e Terra 38
15. Membra Arborum 40
16. Arbores Silvestres 42
17. Nuces et Bacae 44

18. Genera Florum. 46
19. Poma 48
20. Holera et Legumina. 50
21. Condimenta 52
22. Corpus 54
23. Caput et Facies 56
24. Manus et Pes. 58
25. Membra Interiora Corporis 60
26. Ossa 62
27. Terra 64
28. Mare. 66
29. Dies et Nox 68
30. Tempestas Caeli. 70
31. Genera Terrae 72
32. Membra Floris et Frumenti 74
   Glossary 77
   Appendix of Declensions 99

INTRODUCTION

Commenius' *Orbis Pictus*

The *Orbis Pictus* series is a new twist on a 350-year-old idea for teaching Latin. The namesake and inspiration for this new textbook is a work of the celebrated educator, John Amos Commenius (1592-1670), called *Orbis Pictus* or *Orbis Sensualium Pictus* ("The Visible World in Pictures"). This book is considered to have been the first children's picture book. It was first printed in 1658 in Nuremberg in Latin and German, subsequently translated into numerous languages, and widely used throughout world for over two hundred years.

The original *Orbis Pictus* was designed to be a child's first Latin textbook and introduced vocabulary to beginning students (about twelve or thirteen years old) through 150 chapters on every topic from the nature of God to the water cycle to species of birds to a cobbler's workshop. Each chapter contained illustrations of the vocabulary to be taught and very simple narrative in both Latin and a student's mother tongue in parallel columns.

Commenius produced this textbook in part to correct problems with how students were learning Latin vocabulary in his day: students were either 1) learning lists of Latin vocabulary (often from a dictionary) along with their definitions, or 2) hoping to build up vocabulary naturally by reading Latin texts. He criticizes the first practice, pointing out that students who learn lists of vocabulary frequently do not fully understand the concepts themselves behind the words. He likens a person who tries to learn vocabulary in such a way to one who "hopes he can gather the sand of the seashore with his bare hands." He allows that the second method (learning vocabulary by wide reading) is possible, but points out that it is inefficient since a student only encounters vocabulary at random when reading. As he put it, "It would be much easier for one to learn to distinguish all the animals by sight by visiting Noah's ark . . . than to travel to the whole world until he has chanced upon every animal."

Commenius' *Orbis Pictus* was designed to improve upon these two methods, 1) by giving illustrations and context for each new word so students could understand exactly what it was referring to, and 2) by systematizing vocabulary by topic. Although modern Latin textbooks have made great strides in introducing basic Latin grammar to students, modern classrooms have largely fallen into these same two pitfalls when teaching new vocabulary. The result is that students who have studied Latin for many years often lack even a rudimentary knowledge of Latin vocabulary. This is a travesty, considering that knowledge of Latin vocabulary bears the most immediate fruit for a modern student of Latin.

Since Commenius' method was so effective in improving the instruction of Latin vocabulary in the seventeenth century, I have generally sought to follow his example in the construction of this textbook. However, in order to be more useful to a modern audience, I have made a few significant changes.

First, I have not attempted to be exhaustive. The original *Orbis Pictus* is daunting to the modern student for the sheer number of vocabulary it introduces (upwards of ten thousand). I have sought instead to include only the words most common in Latin texts, words that are frequently used in biology, and words for things modern students are most likely to want to know (e.g., *taraxacum,* "dandelion").

Second, I have used macaronic (English mixed with Latin) instead of straight English for the vernacular column. This is to allow a student to pick up Latin vocabulary from context without having any prior knowledge of Latin. The English equivalents for each Latin word are included, but only in an appendix. This encourages a student to figure the meaning of the word out from the picture provided or context.

Third, I have included wherever possible something axiomatic about the concept the word refers to, in order both to present a handle to aid a student's memory, and also to help younger students better understand the concept that the word represents.

Lastly, I have not attempted to encompass every topic in one volume. The first volume contains topics concerning the natural world. The second will focus on Greco-Roman society with chapters on war, agriculture, clothing, etc. Subsequent volumes will likely focus on medieval and modern society.

Methodology

Although Latin has been remarkably stable for over two millennia, there have been significant changes in its vocabulary and word order. It is consequently impossible to choose a perfect general vocabulary or composition style, especially considering the broad goals of this textbook. I have attempted to do what is most useful for a general student of Latin and will doubtless offend purists in every camp.

In regard to word order, even a beginning student of Latin may notice that I do not follow the style of Cicero and other orators that has become accepted as "authentic." The truth is that authentic Latin is extraordinarily flexible in this regard. I have deliberately taken advantage of this to make my parallel columns in English and Latin as like as possible. Although the style of both the English and Latin is consequently somewhat affected, there is a clear pedagogical advantage to using a similar word order: even the most elementary student may find the English equivalents of the Latin column by reading it as they would an interlinear text.

Whenever practical I have selected words and spellings used in the classical period. Where synonyms exist, I have chosen what seems most popular in the surviving literature. Because his usage is more precise, I often preferred words found in Pliny the Elder's *Natural Histories* to those used by the poets and orators. Additionally, since this book seeks to aid a student's comprehension of modern technical terminology, I have preferred words later adopted in the scientific community. When absolutely necessary I have used neo-Latin words, which are clearly designated with an asterisk. For teachers who object to my vocabulary choice, I would encourage them to simply change it. I have included a list of possible alternatives in the glossary.

Orbis Pictus Users' Guide

This textbook is not designed to replace a teacher. It is a merely a tool, but one flexible enough to aid anyone teaching or learning Latin at any level. As such, it contains no schedules, worksheets, quizzes, or instruction for students. Teachers, parents, and those learning Latin on their own should use it in such a way and at such a pace that best meets their needs. That said, I have included some general guidelines.

For Beginning Students

The Natural World is divided into thirty-two chapters, and every chapter is focused on some area of the natural world. Each chapter is organized into four parts: the picture, the word list, the macaronic sentences, and the Latin sentences.

Specific vocabulary concepts in a given chapter are marked with a lowercase Roman numeral. By matching numerals, a student can find the specific Latin word for the concept in the vocabulary list, which is located under the picture. The numeral also matches the macaronic sentence (located in the left-hand column) which describes, specifies, and contextualizes the vocabulary word.

In the right-hand column, the student will find Latin translations of the macaronic sentences. I have preserved word order between the sentences to allow the reader to refer back to the macaronic sentences, if stumped by the Latin. Should a reader need further help, all the vocabulary for the chapters is found in the back of the book, along with English definitions and pronunciation help for singular and plural forms. Also included in the glossary at the back are extra words which could crop up during the study of a given chapter.

Students that cannot yet read Latin should ignore the right-hand column entirely and begin instead with the macaronic story in the left-hand column. As they come to Latin words, they should try to guess from context what they mean. This can be done as a class or individually. They should also be encouraged to refer to the pictures on the left-hand page. Once students have made their way through the entire column by going back and forth between the macaronic text and the pictures, they should quiz themselves on the pictures alone. Once students have mastered all the words in the chapter this way, a teacher or parent may quiz them in two ways: a teacher may point out the pictures in the book, or she may read the macaronic text aloud, and allow students to fill in the Latin words. This kind of quiz can be oral or written. Ideally, it would be done orally first, then written. These exercises can be done one after another in a day or stretched out over an extended period of time. It is normally difficult to learn more than one chapter of vocabulary per week.

In the case of younger students, it is highly recommended to spend some time talking about the concept behind each Latin word. For instance, once a third-grader (or a class of third-graders) makes the realization that *aquila* means "eagle," try asking what he knows about eagles. Then, have a discussion about it. Anyone that has ever taught elementary or junior-high students knows how much they love discussions. Discussions of this sort are not tangents—thinking about the concept will solidify what the word really signifies.

For Advanced Students

The right-hand column is designed for students who already know Latin grammar and can read Latin prose. They should begin by reading slowly through the right-hand column. If they prefer, they can first use the pictures and labels to learn the major vocabulary. When they come to unfamiliar words in the text, they should first attempt to figure them out from context. If they cannot, they can look at the pictures or the left-hand column to see what a word or phrase means. Once they have made it through the entire column once slowly, they should read over it several times to make sure they remember all the words. Advanced students can be quizzed in the same way as beginning students. Additionally, they can be assigned to retranslate the English column into Latin without referring to the Latin column. They can also write a Latin composition using some of the new vocabulary.

As a Stand-Alone

Latin vocabulary is useful on its own. Even without learning the grammar and language, a student can learn how words work, learn Latin roots for English and the Romance languages, and build a foundation for scientific terminology. If students only wish to work on vocabulary roots, they may use the Orbis Pictus series without ever learning the grammar.

In Combination with Another Textbook

If the students are working through another textbook, vocabulary with *The Natural World* can serve as a welcome break to the students' chanting, translating, or reading. However, since other textbooks may use different vocabulary, it is recommended that a teacher replace words throughout *The Natural World* to make the vocabularies consistent.

ORBIS PICTUS
The Natural World

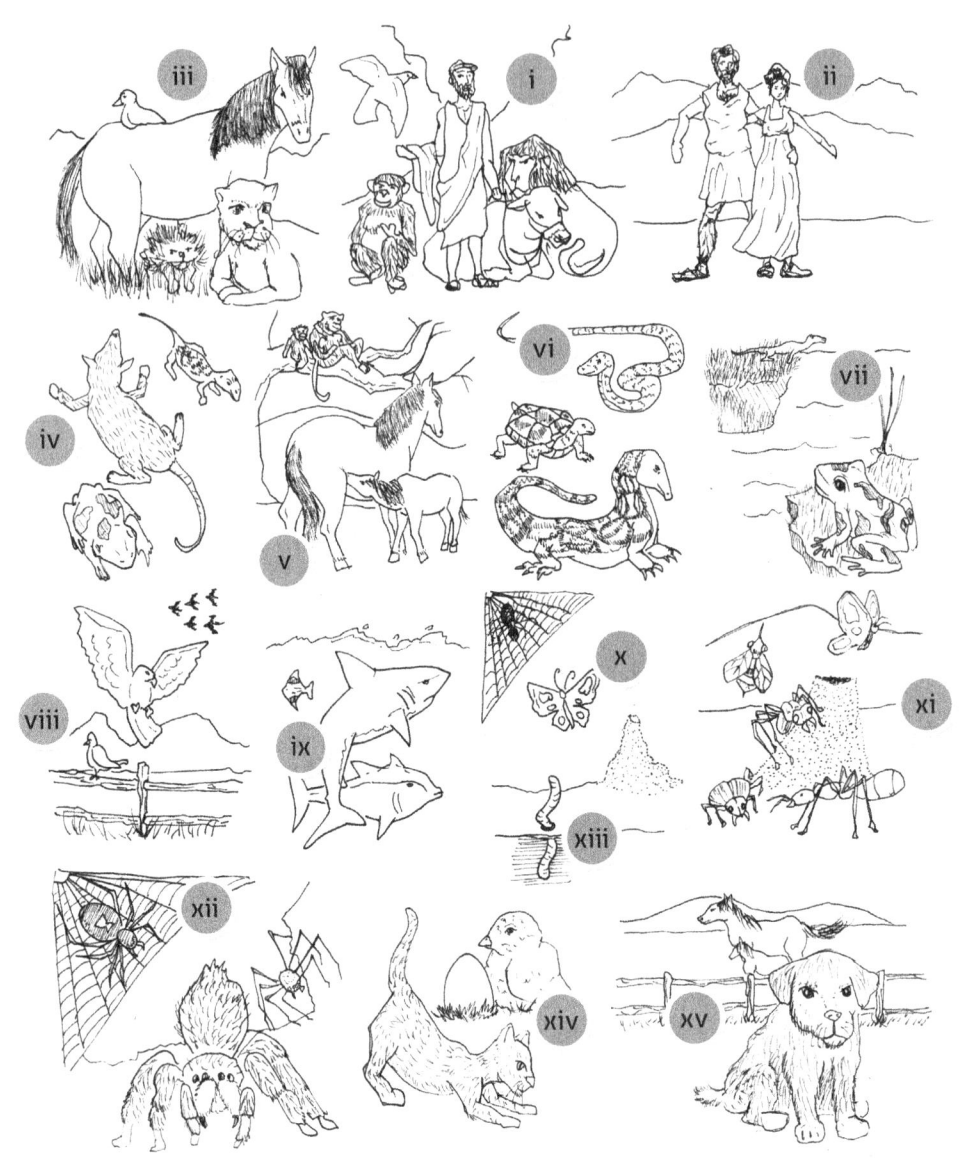

CH. 1 WORD LIST

i. animal, animālis, n.
ii. homo, hominis, c.
iii. bestia, -ae, f.
iv. quādrupēs, quādrupedis, f.
v. mammal, mammālis, n.
vi. reptile, -is, n.
vii. amphibion,* -ī, n.
viii. avis, -is, f.
ix. piscis, -is, m.
x. bestiola, -ae, f.
xi. insectum, -ī, n.
xii. arānea, -ae, f.
xiii. vermis, -is, m.
xiv. pullus, -ī, m.
xv. catulus, -ī, m.

GENERA ANIMALIUM

Ch. 1

Whatever draws breath is called an *animal*. (i)

The *animal* that rules the world is the *homo*. (ii) All other *animālia* are also called *bestiae*. (iii)

An *animal* that has four feet is called a *quādrupēs*. (iv)

A *quādrupēs* that feeds its young with milk is called a *mammal*. (v)

A *quādrupēs* that crawls on its belly is called a *reptile*. (vi)

A *quādrupēs* that lives both in water and on land is called an *amphibion*. (vii)

An *animal* that has two feet and two wings is called an *avis*. (viii)

An *animal* with fins and a tail that lives in the water is called a *piscis*. (ix)

A very small *bestia* is called a *bestiola*. (x)

A *bestiola* with six legs is called an *insectum*. (xi)

A *bestiola* with eight legs that weaves webs is called an *arānea*. (xii)

A *bestiola* without legs that crawls on the ground is called a *vermis*. (xiii)

The young of any *animal*, but especially of an *avis*, is called a *pullus*. (xiv)

The young of a *quādrupēs* is also called a *catulus*. (xv)

Quidquid dūcit animam appellātur *animal*.

Animal quod regit orbem terrārum est *homo*. Omnia alia *animālia* etiam appellantur *bestiae*.

Animal cui sunt quattuor pedēs appellātur *quādrupēs*.

Quādrupēs quae alit prōlem lacte appellātur *mammal*.

Quādrupēs quae rēpit super ventrem appellātur *reptile*.

Quādrupēs quae habitat et in aquā et in terrā appellātur *amphibion*.

Animal cui sunt duo pedēs et duae alae appellātur *avis*.

Animal cum pinnīs et caudā quod habitat in aquā appellātur *piscis*.

Exigua *bestia* appellātur *bestiola*.

Bestiola cum sex pedibus appellātur *insectum*.

Bestiola cum octō pedibus quae tēxit tēlās appellātur *arānea*.

Bestiola sine pedibus quae rēpit in terrā appellātur *vermis*.

Prōlēs cuiusvīs *animālis* sed maximē *avis* appellātur *pullus*.

Prōlēs *quādrupedis* etiam appellātur *catulus*.

CH. 2 WORD LIST

i. pilus, -ī, m.
ii. villus, -ī, m.
iii. lāna, -ae, f.
iv. saeta, -ae, f.
v. iuba, -ae, f.
vi. acūleus, -ī, m.
vii. cutis, -is, f.
viii. pellis, -is, f.
ix. corium, -ī, n.
x. testa, -ae, f.
xi. cornū, -ūs, n.
xii. dens, dentis, m.
xiii. unguis, -is, f.
xiv. ungula, -ae, f.

MEMBRA QUADRUPEDIS
Ch. 2

Men and many beasts are covered in *pilus*. (i)

The thick *pilus* that covers beasts is called *villus*. (ii)

The soft *villus* that covers sheep and a few other animals is called *lāna*. (iii)

The stiff *pilus* that covers pigs and is in mens' beards is called *saeta*. (iv)

The long *villus* on the necks of lions and horses neck is called a *iuba*. (v)

The long sharp *pilī* on porcupines and hedgehogs are called *aculeī*. (vi)

The outer part of a body is called *cutis*. (vii) An animal's *cutis* is also called *pellis*. (viii)

The thick, tough *pellis* that covers cows, elephants, hippopotamuses, and other animals is called *corium*. (ix)

The very rough and hard *pellis* of a turtle is called a *testa*. (x)

Deer, cows, rhinoceroses, and many other animals have long pointed *cornua* (xi) protruding from their heads.

Boars and elephants have long *dentēs* (xii) protruding from above their mouths.

Men and animals have *unguēs* (xiii) at the ends of their hands and feet.

Horses, cows, and other animals have round *unguēs* called *ungulae*. (xiv)

Hominēs et multae bestiae teguntur *pilō*.

Densus *pilus* quī operit bestiās appellātur *villus*.

Mollis *villus* quī tegit ovēs et nonnullās aliās bestiās appellātur *lāna*.

Rigidus *pilus* quī tegit porcōs et est in virōrum barbīs appellātur *saeta*.

Longus *villus* in cervicibus leōnum et equōrum appellātur *iuba*.

Longī et acūtī *pilī* in hystricibus et ērināceīs appellantur *aculeī*.

Exterior pars corporis appellātur *cutis*. Bestiae *cutis* etiam appellātur *pellis*.

Crassa dūraque *pellis* quae tegit bovēs, elephantēs, hippopotamōs, et aliās bestiās appellātur *corium*.

Aspera et dūra *pellis* testūdinis appellātur *testa*.

Cervīs, bōbus, rhīnocerōtibus, et multīs aliīs bestiīs sunt longa acūtaque *cornua* ēminentia ex capitibus.

Aprīs et elephantibus sunt longī *dentēs* ēminentēs suprā ōra.

Hominibus et bestiīs sunt *unguēs* in extrēmīs manibus et pedibus.

Equīs, bōbus, et aliīs bestiīs sunt rotundae *unguēs* appellātae *ungulae*.

CH. 3 WORD LIST

i. branchiae, -ārum, f. pl.
ii. cauda, -ae, f.
iii. dorsum, -ī, n.
iv. pinna, -ae, f.
v. squāma, -ae, f.
vi. spīna, -ae, f.
vii. āla, -ae, f.
viii. penna, -ae, f.
ix. plūma, -ae, f.
x. rōstrum, -ī, n.
xi. crista, -ae, f.
xii. ōvum, -ī, n.
xiii. nīdus, -ī, m.
xiv. testa, -ae, f.
xv. vitellus, -ī, m.
xvi. albūmen, albūminis, n.

MEMBRA PISCIS ET AVIS

Ch. 3

A fish has no lungs, but instead breathes with *branchiae*. ⓘ

A fish does not walk and has no legs, but instead swims with its *cauda*. ⓘⓘ

The top of a fish is called a *dorsum*. ⓘⓘⓘ A swimming fish changes its direction with its *pennae*, ⓘᵥ which are on its sides and *dorsum*.

Some fish are completely covered in hard *squāmae*. ᵥ

Some have sharp *spīnae* ᵥⓘ on their *dorsum*.

A bird walks on two feet and flies with two *alae*. ᵥⓘⓘ

On top, a bird is covered in long, stiff *pennae*. ᵥⓘⓘⓘ Underneath, it is covered in short, soft *plūmae*. ⓘₓ

In place of a mouth, a bird has a hard *rōstrum*. ₓ

On top of the head, some birds have a colorful *crista*. ₓⓘ

Both fish and birds lay *ōva:* ₓⓘⓘ fish lay soft *ōva* in the water, birds lay hard *ōva* in a *nīdus*. ₓⓘⓘⓘ

The *ōvum* of a bird is covered in a hard *testa*. ₓⓘᵥ

Inside is the yellow *vitellus* ₓᵥ and the white *albūmen*. ₓᵥⓘ

Piscis nōn habet pulmōnēs, sed potius spīrat *branchiīs*.

Piscis nōn ambulat neque habet pedēs, sed potius natat *caudā*.

Summa pars piscis appellātur *dorsum*. Natāns piscis flectit cursum *pennīs*, quae sunt in lateribus et *dorsō*.

Aliī piscēs omnīnō operīuntur dūrīs *squāmīs*.

Aliīs sunt acūtae *spīnae* super *dorsum*.

Avis ambulat duōbus pedibus et volat duābus *alīs*.

Insuper avis tegitur longīs rigidīs *pennīs*. Subter, tegitur brevibus mollibus *plūmīs*.

In locō ōris avis habet dūrum *rōstrum*.

In summō capite aliae avēs habent multicolorem *cristam*.

Et piscēs et avēs pariunt *ōva*: piscēs pariunt mollia *ōva* in aquā, avēs pariunt dūra ōva in *nīdō*.

Ōvum avis tegitur dūrā *testā*.

Intus est lūteus *vitellus* et album *albūmen*.

CH. 4 WORD LIST

i. canis, -is, c.
ii. fēles, -is, f.
iii. bōs, bovis, c.
iv. vacca, -ae, f.
v. taurus, -ī, m.
vi. vitulus, -ī, m.
vii. ovis, -is, f.
viii. ariēs, ariētis, m.
ix. agnus, -ī, m.
x. hircus, -ī, m.
xi. equus, -ī, m.
xii. equulus, -ī, m.
xiii. asinus, -ī, m.
xiv. sūs, suis, c.
xv. porca, -ae, f.
xvi. porcellus, -ī, m.
xvii. gallīna, -ae, f.
xviii. gallus, -ī, m.
xix. pullus gallīnāceus, -ī, m.
xx. anas, anatis, f.

BESTIAE MANSUETAE
Ch. 4

The watcher of the home is the *canis*, (i) which barks, howls, and carries back sticks to its master.

The house is rid of mice by the *fēles*, (ii) which mews and purrs.

The largest of the tame animals is the *bōs*, (iii) which moos. The female is called a *vacca*, (iv) which people milk. The male is called a *taurus*, (v) which when angry attacks with its horns. The baby is called the *vitulus*, (vi) which skips and kicks in the field.

The stupidest of animals is the *ovis*, (vii) which bleats and is covered in wool. The male is called the *ariēs*, (viii) which charges with its horns. The baby *ovis* is called the *agnus*. (ix)

Larger than the *ovis* is the bearded *hircus*. (x) The female is a *capra*, which people milk to make cheese. The baby is called a *haedus*.

A man is carried on a maned *equus*, (xi) which whinnies and pulls carts, carriages, and chariots. The female is called an *equa*. The baby is called an *equulus*. (xii)

A long-eared *asinus* (xiii) carries burdens.

In the pen, the *sūs* (xiv) digs up the ground with its snout. A male is called a *porcus*, and a female a *porca*. (xv) A baby is called a *porcellus*. (xvi)

In the roost, the *gallīna* (xvii) lays eggs. The male is called a *gallus*, (xviii) which crows and fights with spurs. The baby is called a *pullus gallīnāceus*. (xix)

The *anas*, (xx) which quacks, dips itself.

Custōs domūs est *canis* quī lātrat, ululat, et refert virgulās dominō.

Domus purgātur mūribus a *fēle* quae clāmat et murmurat.

Maxima domesticārum bestiārum est *bōs* quī mugit. Fēmina appellātur *vacca* quam hominēs mulgent. Mās appellātur *taurus* quī irātus petit cornibus. Pullus appellātur *vitulus* quī saltat et calcitrat in campō.

Stultissima bestiārum est *ovis* quae bālat et tegitur lānā. Mās appellātur *ariēs* quī impetum facit cornibus. Pullus *ovis* appellātur *agnus*.

Māior quam *ovis* est barbātus *hircus*. Fēmina est *capra* quam hominēs mulgent ad faciendum cāseum. Pullus appellātur haedus.

Homo vehitur iubātō *equō* quī hinnit atque trahit carrōs, raedās, et currūs. Femina appellātur *equa*. Pullus appellātur *equulus*.

Aurītus *asinus* vehit onera.

In harā *sūs* fodit terram rōstrō. Mās appellātur *porcus*, et fēmina *porca*. Pullus appellātur *porcellus*.

In scalā gallināriā, *gallīna* parit ōva. Mās appellātur *gallus*, quī cucurrit et pugnat calcāribus. Pullus appellātur *pullus gallīnāceus*.

Anas, quī tētrinnit, mergit sē.

20 • ORBIS PICTUS

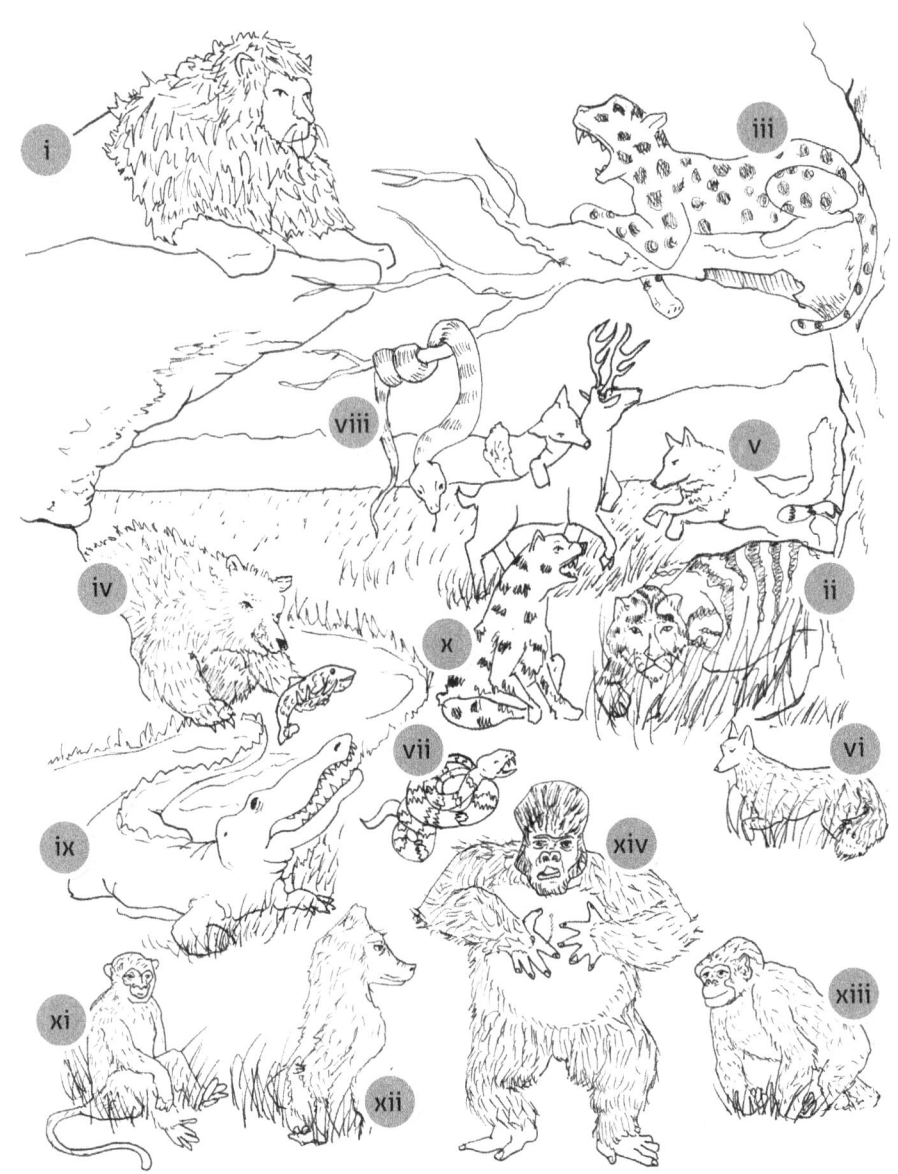

CH. 5 WORD LIST

i. leo, leōnis, m.
ii. tīgris, -is, f.
iii. pardus, -ī, m.
iv. ursus, -ī, m.
v. lupus, -ī, m.
vi. vulpes, -is, f.
vii. anguis, -is, c.
viii. draco, dracōnis, m.
ix. crocodīlus, -ī, m.
x. hyaena, -ae, f.
xi. sīmia, -ae, f.
xii. cynocephalus, -ī, m.
xiii. satyrus, -ī, m.
xiv. gorilla,* -ae, f.

BESTIAE FERAE
Ch. 5

A great mane covers the tawny *leo*, (i) which is called the king of the beasts.

Hidden by its striped body, the savage *tīgris* (ii) hunts in the tall grass.

Spots mark the *pardus*, (iii) which leaps down on its prey from the trees.

Shaggy hair covers the great *ursus*, (iv) which with its sharp teeth catches fish from the river.

Packs of *lupī* (v) chase down deer.

The craftiest of all animals, the long-tailed *vulpes* (vi) evades its pursuers.

Slithering on its belly, the quick *anguis* (vii) kills with venom.

Squeezing with its long coils, the *draco* (viii) crushes its prey and swallows it whole.

Out of the river, the *crocodīlus* (ix) suddenly snatches its prey and drags it to the bottom.

The spotted *hyaena* (x) has a cry like laughter.

The snub-nosed *sīmia* (xi) has a long tail and imitates man's movements.

Similar to the *sīmia* is the *cynocephalus*, (xii) whose muzzle is like a dog's and rear-end is red.

The hairy *satyrus* (xiii) walks on its hands and feet.

The giant *gorilla* (xiv) pounds its chest with its fists.

Magna iuba operit fulvum *leōnem* quī appellātur rēx ferārum.

Occulta virgātō corpore saeva *tīgris* venātur inter procerum grāmen.

Maculae notant *pardum* quī dēsilit in praedam ex arboribus.

Villus operit magnum *ursum* quī acūtīs dentibus capit piscēs ex fluviō.

Grēgēs *lupōrum* persequuntur cervōs.

Astūtissima omnium ferārum caudāta *vulpes* fugit persequentēs.

Serpēns super ventrem, celer *anguis* necat venēnō.

Complectēns longīs orbibus *draco* comprimit praedam et vorat tōtam.

Ex flūmine *crocodīlus* subitō rapit praedam et dētrahit ad fundum.

Maculōsae *hyaenae* est vōx similis cachinnō.

Sīma *sīmia* habet longam caudam et simulat hominis motūs.

Similis *sīmiae* est *cynocephalus* cuius rōstrum est canīnum et natēs rubent.

Pilōsus *satyrus* ambulat manibus et pedibus.

Ingēns *gorilla* percutit pectus pugnīs.

CH. 6 WORD LIST

i. camēlus, -ī, m.
ii. camēlopardus, -ī, m.
iii. aper, aprī, m.
iv. cervus, -ī, m.
v. alcē, -ēs, f.
vi. damma, -ae, f.
vii. elephans, elephantis, m.
viii. rhīnoceros, rhīnocerōtis, m.
ix. hippopotamus, -ī, m.
x. zebra,* -ae, f.
xi. rūpicapra, -ae, f.
xii. strūthio, strūthiōnis, m.

MAGNAE BESTIAE
Ch. 6

In the desert, the *camēlus* (i) with its hump carries great burdens and withstands thirst.

With its long neck, the spotted *camēlopardus* (ii) reaches leaves in the treetops.

Armed with curved tusks, the hairy *aper* (iii) charges.

Adorned with branching horns, the *cervus* (iv) flees swiftly through the forest.

An animal like a *cervus,* but with as large a body as a cow's, is the *alke.* (v)

Adorned with long straight horns, the *damma* (vi) flees swiftly over the plain.

The greatest of all the land beasts, the *elephans* (vii) picks up his food with his long trunk.

Armored with hide and a great horn is the unicorn or *rhīnoceros.* (viii)

In the river lives the *hippopotamus,* (ix) which has a hard hide and very long tusks. It is also called the river-horse.

An animal like a horse or a donkey, but with a striped body, is the *zebra.* (x)

In the mountains, the *rūpicapra* (xi) leaps among the rocks.

The greatest of the birds, the *strūthio* (xii) is not able to fly, but runs quickly.

In arēnīs *camēlus* cum gibbere portat magna onera et perpetitur sitim.

Longō collō maculātus *camēlopardus* attingit folia in cacūminibus.

Armātus curvīs dentibus pilōsus *aper* impetum facit.

Ornātus ramōsīs cornibus *cervus* fugit celeriter per silvam.

Animal simile *cervō* sed tantō corpore quantō bōs est *alkē.*

Ornāta longīs rēctīs cornibus, *damma* fugit celeriter super plānitiem.

Maxima terrestrium bestiārum *elephans* tollit cibum longā probiscide.

Armātus coriō et magnō cornū est ūnicornis vel *rhīnoceros.*

In flūmine habitat *hippopotamus,* cui est dūrum corium atque perlongae dentēs. Etiam appellātur equus fluviatilis.

Animal simile equō vel asinō sed virgātō corpore est *zebra.*

In montibus *rūpicapra* salit per saxa.

Maxima avium *strūthio* nōn potest volāre sed currit celeriter.

24 · ORBIS PICTUS

CH. 7 WORD LIST

i. lepus, leporis, m.
ii. mūs, mūris, m.
iii. sciūrus, -ī, m.
iv. cunīculus, -ī, m.
v. talpa, -ae, f.
vi. fiber, fibrī, m.
vii. lūtra, -ae, f.
viii. ērināceus, -ī, m.
ix. hystrix, hystricis, f.
x. mustēla, -ae, f.
xi. procyon,* procyōnis, m.
xii. mēles, -is, f.
xiii. testūdo, testūdinis, f.
xiv. rāna, -ae, f.
xv. lacerta, -ae, f.

PARVA ANIMALIA
Ch. 7

The long-eared *lepus* (i) flees quickly with its powerful legs.

The *mūs* (ii) invades homes and steals grain and other foods.

Before the winter, the *sciūrus* (iii) stores nuts in the hollow of a tree.

The fearful *cunīculus* (iv) digs up the ground and hides in a deep burrow.

The blind *talpa* (v) makes burrows.

With its long teeth, the *fiber* (vi) fells trees by the river.

Covered in soft hair, the playful *lūtra* (vii) swims in the rivers.

The spiny *ērināceus* (viii) rolls into the shape of a ball to protect itself.

The bristling *hystrix* (ix) shoots long quills at pursuers.

The thin *mustēla* (x) follows *mūrēs* even into their burrows.

With nimble fingers, the *procyon* (xi) washes its food in the river.

With its striped head, the fierce *mēles* (xii) defends its lair.

The slow *testūdō* (xiii) pulls back its head and feet inside its shell.

The leaping *rāna* (xiv) catches flies with its long tongue.

The elusive *lacerta* (xv) tastes the air with its forked tongue.

Aurītus *lepus* fugit celeriter validīs pedibus.

Mūs īnfēstat domum et furātur frūmentum et aliōs cibōs.

Ante hiemem *sciūrus* servat nucēs in cavā arbore.

Pavidus *cunīculus* perfodit terram et latet in altō cunīculō.

Caeca *talpa* facit grumōs.

Longīs dentibus *fiber* caedit arborēs iūxtā flūmen.

Tēcta mollī pilō lascīva *lūtra* natitat in flūminibus.

Spinōsus *ērināceus* convolvitur in formam pilae ad muniendum sē.

Horrida *hystrix* iaculātur longōs aculeōs in persequentēs.

Tenuis *mustēla* sequitur *mūrēs* etiam in cavernās.

Habilibus digitīs *procyon* lavat cibum in flūmine.

Capite virgātō ferōx *mēles* dēfendit suam latebram.

Lenta *testūdō* retrahit caput et pedēs intrā testam.

Saliēns *rāna* capit muscās longā linguā.

Fugax *lacerta* gustat āera bifurcātā linguā.

CH. 8 WORD LIST

i. aquila, -ae, f.
ii. milvus, -ī, f.
iii. accipiter, accipitris, m.
iv. falco, falcōnis, m.
v. vultur, vulturis, m.
vi. būteo, būteōnis, m.
vii. cornix, cornīcis, f.
viii. corvus, -ī, m.
ix. būbo, būbōnis, m.
x. strix, strigis, f.
xi. tytō,* tytois, f.

AVES FERAE

Ch. 8

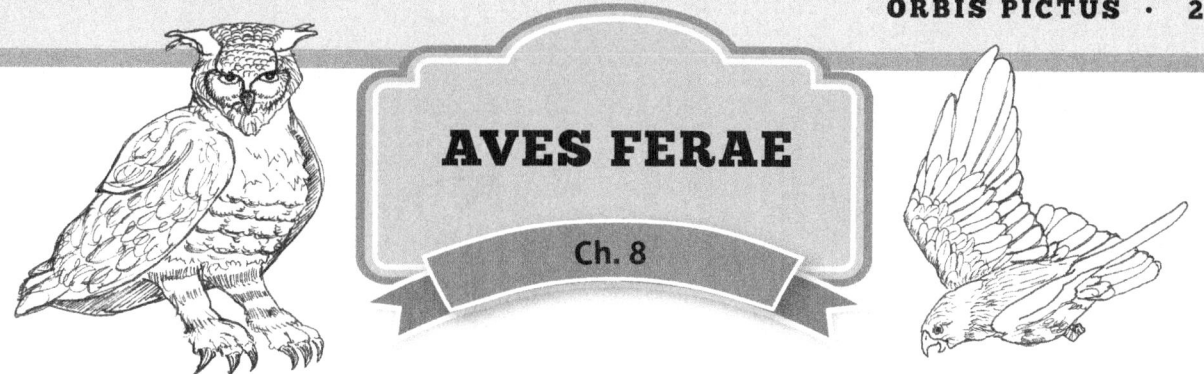

Some birds soaring high in the sky spot small animals on the ground, like the terrifying *aquila*, (i) which is the largest of the flying birds and snatches small animals in its talons;

the soaring *milva*, (ii) which is a little smaller than the *aquila* and has long wings and a wedge-shaped tail;

the merciless *accipiter*, (iii) which hunts birds with men in an alliance;

and the diving *falco*, (iv) which is smaller than the *accipiter* and the quickest of all animals.

Some birds feed on carrion, like the bald *vultur*, (v) which flies in circles;

the powerful *būteo*, (vi) which is smaller than the *vultur* and also catches live prey;

the black *cornix*, (vii) which caws in a hoarse voice;

and the intelligent *corvus*, (viii) which is larger than the *cornix*.

Some birds hunt at night, like the long-eared *būbo*, (ix) which is the largest of the night birds;

the earless *strix*; (x)

and, with a white face in the shape of a heart, the *tytō*. (xi)

Aliae avēs volāntēs in summō caelō cernunt parva animālia in terrā, ut terribilis *aquila* quae est maxima volāntium avium et rapit parva animālia unguibus;

pendens *milva* quae paulō minor quam *aquila* est longīs alīs et cuneātā caudā;

crūdēlis *accipiter* quae aucupātur avēs cum hominibus quādam societāte;

et praecēps *falco* quī est minor quam *accipiter* et celerrimus omnium animālium.

Aliae avēs vescuntur cadāveribus, ut calvus *vultur* quī volat in orbes;

validus *būteo* quī est minor quam *vultur* et etiam capit vīvam praedam;

nigra *cornix* quae crocit raucā vōce;

et prūdens *corvus* quī est māior quam *cornīx*.

Aliae avēs venantur nocte, ut aurītus *būbo* quī est maximus nocturnārum *avium*;

inaurīta *strix*;

et cui est albus vultus formā cordis, *tytō*.

CH. 9 WORD LIST

i. cygnus, -ī, m.
ii. anas, anatis, f.
iii. anser, anseris, m.
iv. grus, gruis, f.
v. ardea, -ae, f.
vi. phoenīcopterus, -ī, m.
vii. cicōnia, -ae, f.
viii. pelicānus, -ī, m.
ix. gavia, -ae, f.
x. haliaetus, -ī, m.
xi. diomedēa,* -ae, f.

AVES AQUATILES

Ch. 9

Some birds swim on top of the water, like the bright white *cygnus*, (i) which is the most beautiful;

the web-footed *anas*, (ii) which quacks and dips itself under the water;

and the loud *anser*, (iii) which honks.

Some birds walk in the shallow water, like the whooping *grus*, (iv) which flies with its long neck outstreched;

the high-flying *ardea*, (v) which flies with its neck pulled back;

the pink *phoenīcopterus*, (vi) which has a hooked beak;

and the voiceless *icōnia*, (vii) which clatters with its bill.

Other birds swooping down snatch fish out of the water with their talons, like the gaping *pelicānus*, (viii) which carries much in its large beak;

the greedy *gavia*, (ix) which glides on the wind near the shore;

a kind of eagle, the *haliaetus*, (x) which searches for fish from the sea;

and, gliding on its huge wings, the *diomedēa*, (xi) which flies with giant wings and follows ships.

Aliae avēs natant super aquam, ut candidus *cygnus* quī est pulcherrimus;

lātipēs *anas* quae tetrinnit et mergit sē sub aquam;

et clāmōsus *anser* quī clangit.

Aliae avēs ambulant in vadīs, ut querula *grus* quae volat longō collō extentō;

sublīmis *ardea* quae volat collō contractō;

roseus *phoenīcopterus* cui est uncum rōstrum;

et mūta *cicōnia* quae crepitat rostrō.

Aliae avēs devolāntēs rapiunt piscēs ex aquā unguibus, ut inhiāns *pelicānus* quī gestat multum in magnō rostrō;

avāra *gavia* quae pendet in ventō prope lītus;

genus aquilae *haliaetus* quī quaerit piscēs ē marī;

et pendens ingentibus alīs *diomedēa* quae volat ingentibus alīs et sequītur navēs.

30 · ORBIS PICTUS

CH. 10 WORD LIST

i. rubecula,* -ae, f.
ii. luscinia, -ae, f.
iii. passer, -is, m.
iv. columba, -ae, f.
v. palumba, -ae, f.
vi. pīcus, -ī, m.
vii. psittacus, -ī, m.
viii. pāvo, pavōnis, m.
ix. cōturnix, cōturnicis, f.
x. tetrao, tetraōnis, m.
xi. phāsiāna, -ae, f.
xii. gallopāvo,* gallopavōnis, m.

AVES ALIAE

Ch. 10

The red *rubecula* (i) looks for earthworms in the grass.

Day and night, the *luscinia* (ii) sings a changing tune.

The most common of birds is the tiny *passer*, (iii) whose feathers are brown and grey.

The peaceful *columba* (iv) coos and bills with her mate.

A kind of *columba*, the *palumba* (v) turns about its colorful neck.

The pecking *pīcus* (vi) looks for bugs in the bark of trees.

The exotic *psittacus* (vii) imitates the voice of a person.

The prideful *pāvo* (viii) has feathers with eyes.

The round *cōturnix* (ix) is hard to see because it hides in the tall grass.

The fearful *tetrao* (x) suddenly takes flight with loud flapping of its wings.

The colorful *phāsiāna* (xi) has long feathers in his tail.

The bearded *gallopāvo* (xii) spreads the feathers in its tail like a fan.

Rubra *rubecula* quaerit lumbricōs in grāmine.

Diē et nocte *luscinia* canit varium carmen.

Frequentissima avium est parvus *passer* cui pennae sunt fuscae et cinereae.

Imbellis *columba* gemit et exosculātur amāntem.

Genus columbae, *palumba* torquet pictum collum.

Tundēns *pīcus* quaerit bestiolās in cortice arborum.

Peregrīnus *psittacus* imitātur vōcem hominis.

Superbō *pāvōnī* sunt pennae oculātae.

Rotunda *cōturnix* est difficilis visū quīa latet in prōcērō grāmine.

Pavida *tetrao* subitō capit fugam strepitū alarum.

Multicolorī *phāsiānae* sunt longae pennae in caudā.

Barbātus *gallopāvo* pandit pennās caudae in speciem flabellī.

CH. 11 WORD LIST

i. bālaena, -ae, f.
ii. cētus, -i, m.
iii. delphīnus, -i, m.
iv. phōca, -ae, f.
v. squalus, -i, m.
vi. pōlypus, -i, m.
vii. sēpia, -ae, f.
viii. urtīca, -ae, f.
ix. lōcusta, -ae, f.
x. cancer, cancrī, m.
xi. concha, -ae, f.

BESTIAE MARINAE
Ch. 11

The greatest of the animals of the sea is the *bālaena*, (i) which breaches the waves and spouts water from its blowhole.

Fiercer is the *cētus*, (ii) which fishermen once hunted for the spermaceti in its giant head.

The most playful and friendliest to men is the *delphīnus*, (iii) which sometimes even carries them on its back.

The swift *phōca*, (iv) which lives both on land and at sea, barks like a dog.

The most terrifying to men is the *squalus* (v) because of its many teeth and its love for blood.

With its eight tentacles the soft *pōlypus* (vi) swims, hunts, and climbs ashore.

With its black ink the many-tentacled *sēpia* (vii) confuses its enemies and flees.

Swimming by contracting itself, the stinging *urtīca* (viii) spreads its hairs to catch little fish and swallows them.

Protected by a fragile shell is the *lōcusta*, (ix) which has long thin antenae which feel out its way, and giant claws which pinch.

A constellation gets its name from the *cancer*, (x) which walks sideways.

A hard shell covers the various kinds of *conchae*, (xi) of which some produce pearls, others purple dye.

Maximum animālium marīnōrum est *bālaena* quae ēmergit ex undīs et ēiicit aquam ex spīrāculō.

Ferōcior est *cētus* quem piscātōrēs olim vēnābantur ob sperma cētī in ingentī capite.

Maximē lascīvus et amīcus hominibus est *delphīnus* quī interdum etiam vehit eōs super dorsum.

Celeris *phōca* quae habitat et in terrā et in marī latrat tamquam canis.

Maximē terribilis hominibus est *squalus* ob multōs dentēs et cupidinem sanguinis.

Octo tentāculīs mollis *pōlypus* natat, venātur, et ēgreditur in terram.

Ātrāmentō frondōsa *sēpia* confundit hostēs et aufugit.

Natāns contrahendō sē mordax *urtīca* spargit frondem ut capiat pisciculōs, atque vorat eōs.

Mūnīta fragilī crustā est *lōcusta* cui sunt longa tenuia cornua quae perīclitant viam, et ingentēs chēlās quae vellicant.

Constellātio trahit nōmen ā *cancrō* quī cēdit transversus.

Dūra testa tegit varia genera *conchārum* quārum aliae gignunt margarītās, aliae purpuram.

CH. 12 WORD LIST

i. apis, -is, f.
ii. formīca, -ae, f.
iii. musca, -ae, f.
iv. vespa, -ae, f.
v. cicāda, -ae, f.
vi. gryllus, -i, m.
vii. arānea, -ae, f.
viii. centipeda, -ae, f.
ix. libella,* -ae, f.
x. ērūca, -ae, f.
xi. lumbrīcus, -i, m.
xii. culex, culicis, m.
xiii. ricinus, -i, m.
xiv. scarabaeus, -i, m.
xv. vermīculus, -i, m.
xvi. pāpilio, pāpiliōnis, m.
xvii. tinea, -ae, f.
xviii. blatta, -ae, f.

BESTIOLAE
Ch. 12

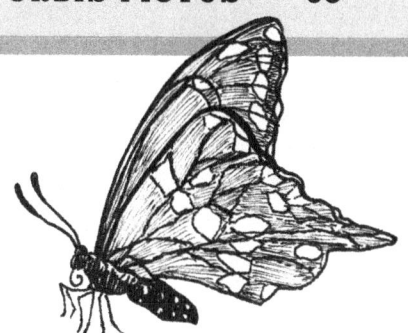

The busy *apis* (i) makes honey.

The hard-working *formīca* (ii) stores up food in a mound of dirt.

The irritating *musca* (iii) flies about in the house.

The angry *vespa* (iv) makes nests and pricks people with its stinger.

The leaping *cicāda* (v) gnaws on crops.

The nocturnal *gryllus* (vi) chirps.

The crafty *arānea* (vii) weaves webs.

The long *centipeda* (viii) has many feet.

The bright-colored *libella* (ix) hovers in the air above swamps and ponds.

The hungry *ērūca* (x) eats leaves and wraps itself in a chrysallis.

The writhing *lumbrīcus* (xi) digs the earth.

The whining *culex* (xii) bites man and flies away.

The blood-sucking *ricinus* (xiii) buries its head under the skin.

The gnawing *scarabaeus* (xiv) covers its wings with a sheath.

The white *vermīculus* (xv) feeds on the flesh of carrion.

The great-winged *pāpilio* (xvi) drinks the nectar of flowers.

The chewing *tinea* (xvii) ruins clothing.

The foul *blatta* (xviii) runs from light.

Negōtiōsa *apis* facit mel.

Industria *formīca* servat cibum in grūmulō.

Molesta *musca* volitat in domō.

Īrācunda *vespa* facit nīdōs et percutit hominēs acūleō.

Saltātrix *cicāda* rōdit frūgēs.

Nocturnus *gryllus* strīdet.

Subdola *arānea* texit tēlās.

Longae *centipedae* sunt multī pedēs.

Picta *libella* pendet in āere super palūdēs et stagna.

Vorax *ērūca* rōdit folia et involvit sē chrysallide.

Sinuāns *lumbrīcus* fodit terram.

Murmurāns *culex* percutit hominēs et āvolat.

Sanguisūgus *ricinus* condit caput sub cute.

Ērōdēns *scarabaeus* tegit pinnulās tegimine.

Albus *vermīculus* vescitur carne cadāverum.

Alātus *pāpilio* bibit sūcum ex flōribus.

Edax *tinea* perdit vestīmenta.

Turpis *blatta* fugit lūcem.

36 · ORBIS PICTUS

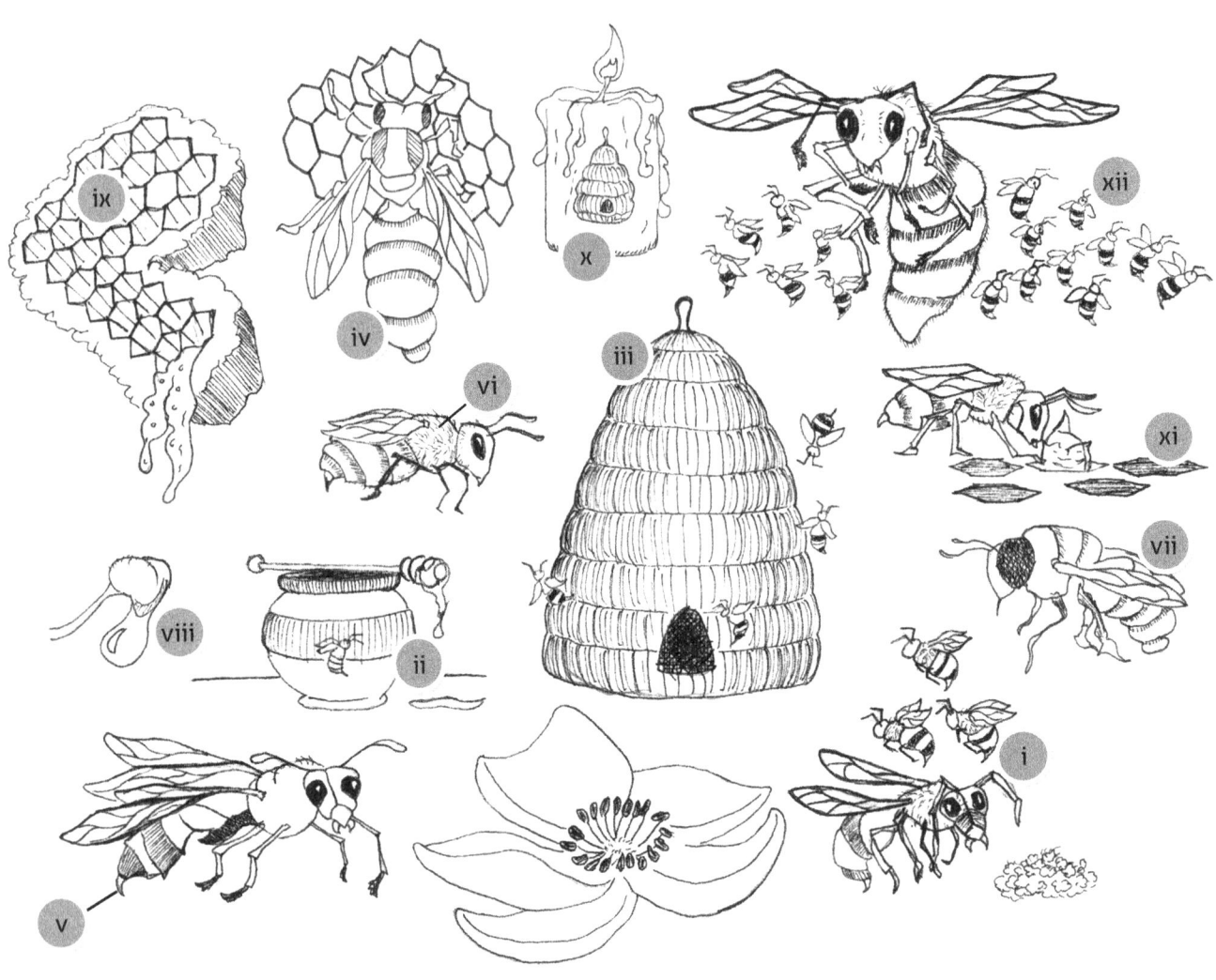

CH. 13 WORD LIST

i. apis, -is, f.
ii. mel, mellis, n.
iii. alvus, -ī, f.
iv. rēgīna,* -ae, f.
v. acūleus, -ī, m.
vi. lānūgo, lānūginis, f.
vii. fūcus, -ī, m.
viii. sūcus, -ī, m.
ix. favus, -ī, m.
x. cera, -ae, f.
xi. cella, -ae, f.
xii. exāmen, exāminis, n.

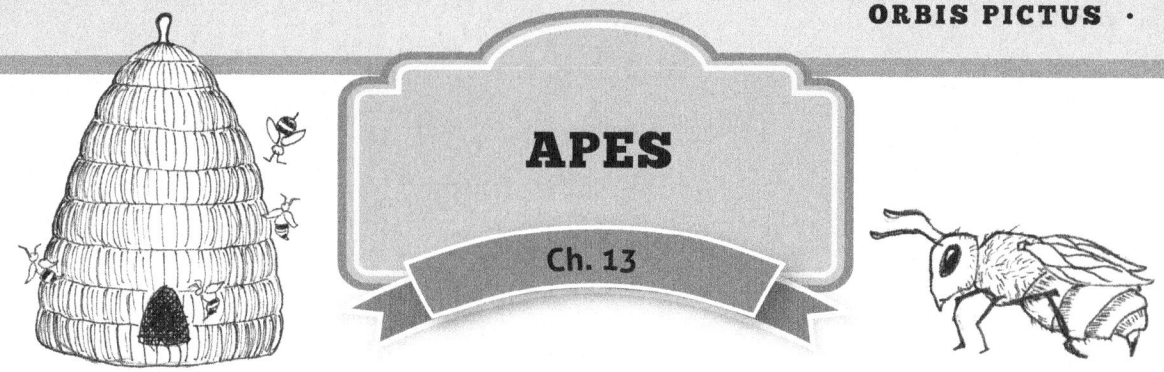

APES

Ch. 13

Most amazing of all the insects is the industrious *apis*, [i] which buzzes and makes sweet *mel*. [ii]

Apēs have a community and live inside one large *alvus*. [iii]

The mother of the *apēs*, which is bigger than the others, is called the *rēgīna*. [iv]

A female *apis*, which has a venomous *acūleus* [v] in the back and soft *lānūgo* [vi] all over her body, goes out to work among the flowers.

A male *apis*, which has large eyes and no *acūleus*, is called a *fūcus*. [vii]

An *apis* sits on a flower and collects *sūcus* [viii] with its mouth, legs, and *lānūgo*. Then it carries it back to the *alvus*.

Inside the *alvus*, the *apis* builds a *favus* [ix] out of soft *cera*. [x]

In the *favus* are many *cellae*, [xi] which have six sides. *Apēs* fill up the *cellae*: some with *mel*, others with larvae.

At certain times in the year, all the *apēs* fly out of the *alvus* and make an *exāmen*. [xii]

Maximē mīrābilis ex insectīs est industria *apis* quae bombītat et facit dulce *mel*.

Apēs habent rem publicam et habitant intrā unam magnam *alvum*.

Māter *apium* quae est māior quam cēterae appellātur *rēgīna*.

Fēmina *apis* cui est venēnōsus *acūleus* in posteriōrī atque mollis *lānūgo* per tōtum corpus exit ad opera inter flōrēs.

Mās *apis* cui sunt magnī oculī et nullus *acūleus* appellātur *fūcus*.

Apis insedit in flōre et colligit *sūcum* ōre, pedibus, et *lānūgine*. Deinde reportat eum ad *alvum*.

Intrā *alvum* apis struit *favum* ex mollī *cerā*.

In *favō* sunt multae *cellae* quibus sunt sex latera. *Apēs* implent *cellās*: aliās *melle*, aliās vermiculīs.

Quibusdam temporibus annī omnēs *apēs* ēvolant ex *alvō* et faciunt *exāmen*.

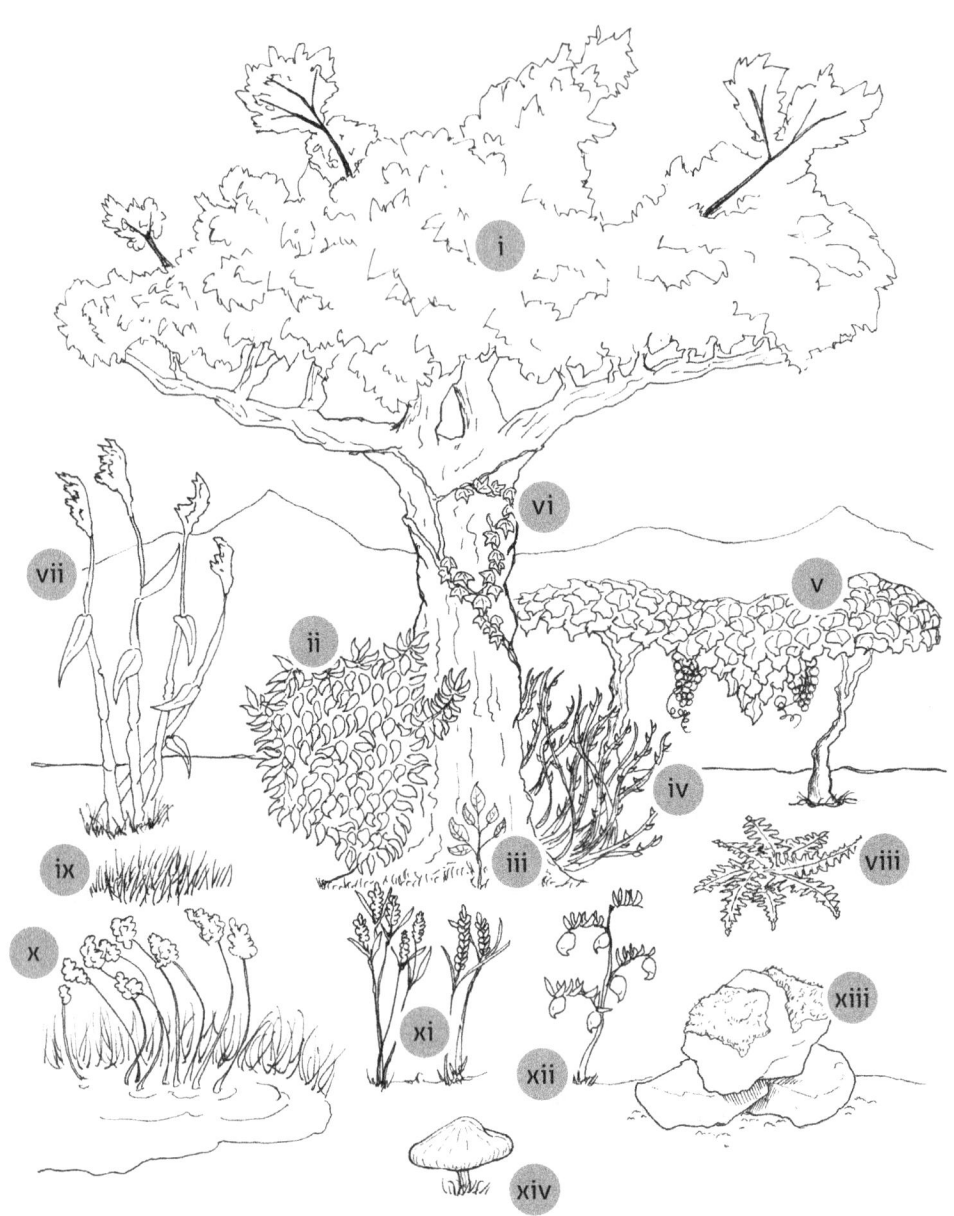

CH. 14 WORD LIST

i. arbor, -is, f.
ii. frutex, fruticis, m.
iii. stirps, stirpis, f.
iv. vēpres, -is, f.
v. vītis, -is, f.
vi. hedera, -ae, f.
vii. harundo, harundinis, f.
viii. filix, filicis, f.
ix. grāmen, grāminis, n.
x. scirpus, -ī, m.
xi. frūmentum, -ī, n.
xii. legūmen, legūminis, n.
xiii. muscus, -ī, m.
xiv. bōlētus, -ī, m.

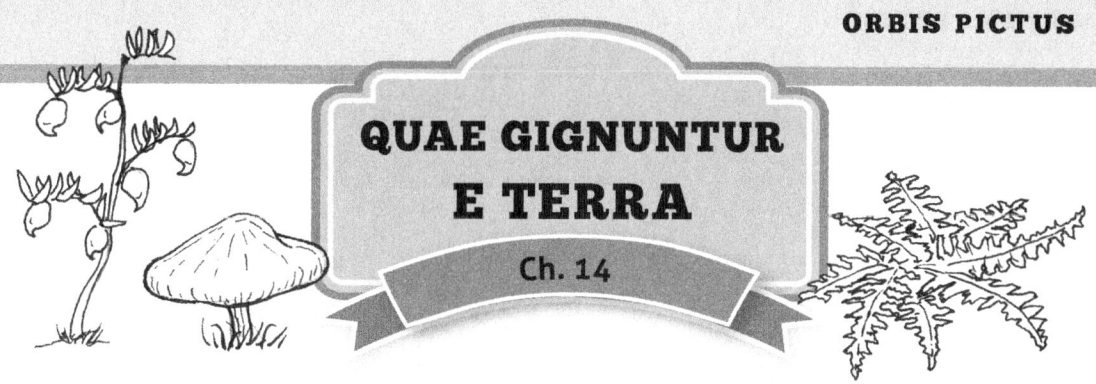

QUAE GIGNUNTUR E TERRA
Ch. 14

These are the things that grow from the ground: the tall *arbor*, (i) which has a long trunk;

the branchy *frutex*, (ii) which is a little smaller than the *arbor*;

the low *stirps*, (iii) which is smaller than the *frutex*;

the tangled *vēpres*, (iv) which bears thorns;

the grapebearing *vītis*, (v) which climbs trees;

the creeping *hedera*, (vi) which is harmful to trees and walls;

the knotty *harundo*, (vii) which has a hollow stem;

the feathery *filix*, (viii) which has divided leaves;

the green *grāmen*, (ix) whose leaves grow from the ground;

the pliant *scirpus*, (x) which is similar to grass but grows by the water;

golden *frūmentum*, (xi) whose fruit is kept in ears;

the windy *legūmen*, (xii) whose fruit is enclosed in pods;

the soft *muscus*, (xiii) which sticks to rocks and trees;

and the often deadly *bōlētus*, (xiv) which stands on one foot.

Haec sunt quae gignuntur ē terrā: procera *arbor* quae est longō truncō;

ramōsa *frutex* quae est paulō minor *arbore*;

humilis *stirps* quae est minor *frutice*;

implicāta *vēpres* quae fert spīnās;

ūvifera *vītis* quae scandit arborēs;

rēpēns *hedera* quae est inimīca arboribus et mūrīs;

geniculāta *harundo* quae est cavā caule;

pinnulāta *filix* cui sunt secta folia;

viride *grāmen* cuius folia oriuntur ē solō;

flexilis *scirpus* quī est similis herbae sed prōvenit apud aquam;

flavescēns *frūmentum* cuius fructus continētur spīcīs;

inflāns *legūmen* cuius fructus inclūditur siliquīs;

mollis *muscus* quī adhaeret saxīs et arboribus;

et saepe mortiferus *bōlētus* quī stat ūnō pede.

CH. 15 WORD LIST

i. rādix, rādīcis, f.
ii. truncus, -ī, m.
iii. cacūmen, cacūminis, n.
iv. rāmus, -ī, m.
v. rāmulus, -ī, m.
vi. folium, -ī, n.
vii. frons, frondis, f.
viii. sēmen, sēminis, n.
ix. cōnus, -ī, m.
x. nux, nucis, -f.
xi. bāca, -ae, f.
xii. acinus, -ī, m.
xiii. cortex, corticis, m.
xiv. lignum, -ī, n.

MEMBRA ARBORIS
Ch. 15

The bottom of a tree is the *rādix*, (i) which supports the tree from under the ground.

The middle of the tree is a large stem that is called the *truncus*. (ii)

The top of the tree above the *truncus* is called the *cacūmen*. (iii)

The *truncus* divides into large *rāmī*. (iv) Out of the *rāmī* grow smaller *rāmī* called *rāmulī*. (v)

From the *rāmulī* hang green *folia*. (vi)

A *rāmulus* together with its *folia* is called a *frons*. (vii)

Among the *folia*, a tree produces *sēmina* (viii) from which new trees grow.

Some trees, like the pine and the fir, produce their *sēmina* in prickly *conī*. (ix)

Some, like the walnut and the oak, produce *sēmina* in hard *nucēs*. (x)

Others, like the olive and the juniper, produce *sēmina* in *bācae*. (xi)

Still others, like the grapevine, produce *acinī*, (xii) which hang in clusters.

The rough outer part of a tree is *cortex*. (xiii) Inside the *cortex* is *lignum*, (xiv) which is useful for making all sorts of things.

Īnfīma arbor est *rādix* quae sustinet arborem sub terrā.

Media arbor est magna stirps quae appellātur *truncus*.

Summa arbor suprā *truncum* appellātur *cacūmen*.

Truncus dīviditur in magnōs *rāmōs*. Ē *rāmīs* crescunt minōrēs *rāmī* appellātī *rāmulī*.

De *rāmulīs* pendent viridia *folia*.

Rāmulus ūnā cum *foliīs* appellātur *frons*.

Inter *folia* arbor fert *sēmina* ex quibus novae arborēs crescunt.

Aliae arborēs ut pīnus et abiēs ferunt *sēmina* in asperīs *conīs*.

Aliae ut iūglāns et glāns ferunt *sēmina* in dūrīs *nucibus*.

Aliae ut olea et iūniperus ferunt *sēmina* in *bācīs*.

Aliae ut *vītis* ferunt *acinōs* quī pedent in racēmīs.

Aspera exterior pars arboris est *cortex*. Intrā *corticem* est *lignum* quod est ūtile ad facienda varia.

CH. 16 WORD LIST

i. quercus, -ūs, f.
ii. rōbur, rōboris, n.
iii. ulmus, -ī, f.
iv. pīnus, -ī, f.
v. abiēs, abietis, f.
vi. platānus, -ī, f.
vii. pōpulus, -ī, f.
viii. acer, aceris, n.
ix. salix, salicis, f.
x. fāgus, -ī, f.
xi. corylus, -ī, f.
xii. fraxinus, -ī, f.
xiii. betula, -ae, f.
xiv. taxus, -ī, f.
xv. tilia, -ae, f.

ARBORES SILVESTRES
Ch. 16

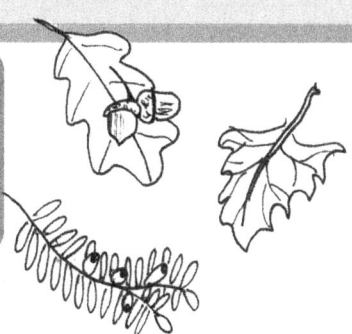

The gnarled *quercus* (i) produces acorns and very hard wood which is called *rōbur*. (ii)

The towering *ulmus* (iii) produces sap useful for glue and wood which does not easily rot when wet.

The branchy *pīnus* (iv) produces a resin called pitch with which torches are made and ships are water-proofed.

Thick with needles, the *abiēs* (v) produces soft and useful lumber.

The great *platānus* (vi) provides pleasing shade.

The tall *pōpulus* (vii) has leaves that shake and white cotton that is carried away by the wind.

The round *ācer* (viii) has beautiful wood and seedpods that fall whirling to the ground.

The bending *salix* (ix) thrives on the riverbanks.

The *fāgus* (x) has fragile and delicate wood, which is useful for burning.

The thickly leafed *corylus* (xi) produces nuts that of their own accord fall out of their husks.

The *fraxinus* (xii) has wood both hard and light, which is most useful for spears.

The *betula* (xiii) has bright white, thin bark.

The deadly *taxus* (xiv) produces poison in its berries, and the strongest bows are made from its wood.

The fragrant *tilia* (xv) attracts bees and has wood useful for sculpting.

Nōdōsa *quercus* fert glandēs et dūrissimum lignum quod appellātur *rōbur*.

Ingēns *ulmus* fert lacrimās ūtilēs ad glūtinum atque lignum quod nōn facile corrumpitur aquā.

Rāmōsa *pīnus* fert rēsīnam nōmine taedam quā facēs efficiuntur et nāvēs illinuntur.

Dēnsa pinnātō foliō *abiēs* fert mollem et ūtilem māteriam.

Grandis *platānus* fert grātam umbram.

Alta *pōpulus* fert folia quae tremunt et candidam lānūginem quae effertur ventō.

Rotundum *ācer* fert pulchrum lignum et siliquās quae cadunt versāntēs ad terram.

Curva *salix* gaudet rīpīs flūminum.

Fāgō est fragile et tenerum lignum quod est ūtile ad cremandum.

Densa foliō *corylus* fert nucēs quae per sē cadunt ē corticibus.

Fraxinus fert lignum et dūrum et leve quod est maximē ūtile ad hastās.

Betulae est candidus et tenuis cortex.

Mortifera *taxus* fert venēnum in bacīs, et validissimī arcūs efficiuntur ēx eius lignō.

Odōra *tilia* allicit apēs et fert lignum ūtile ad sculptūram.

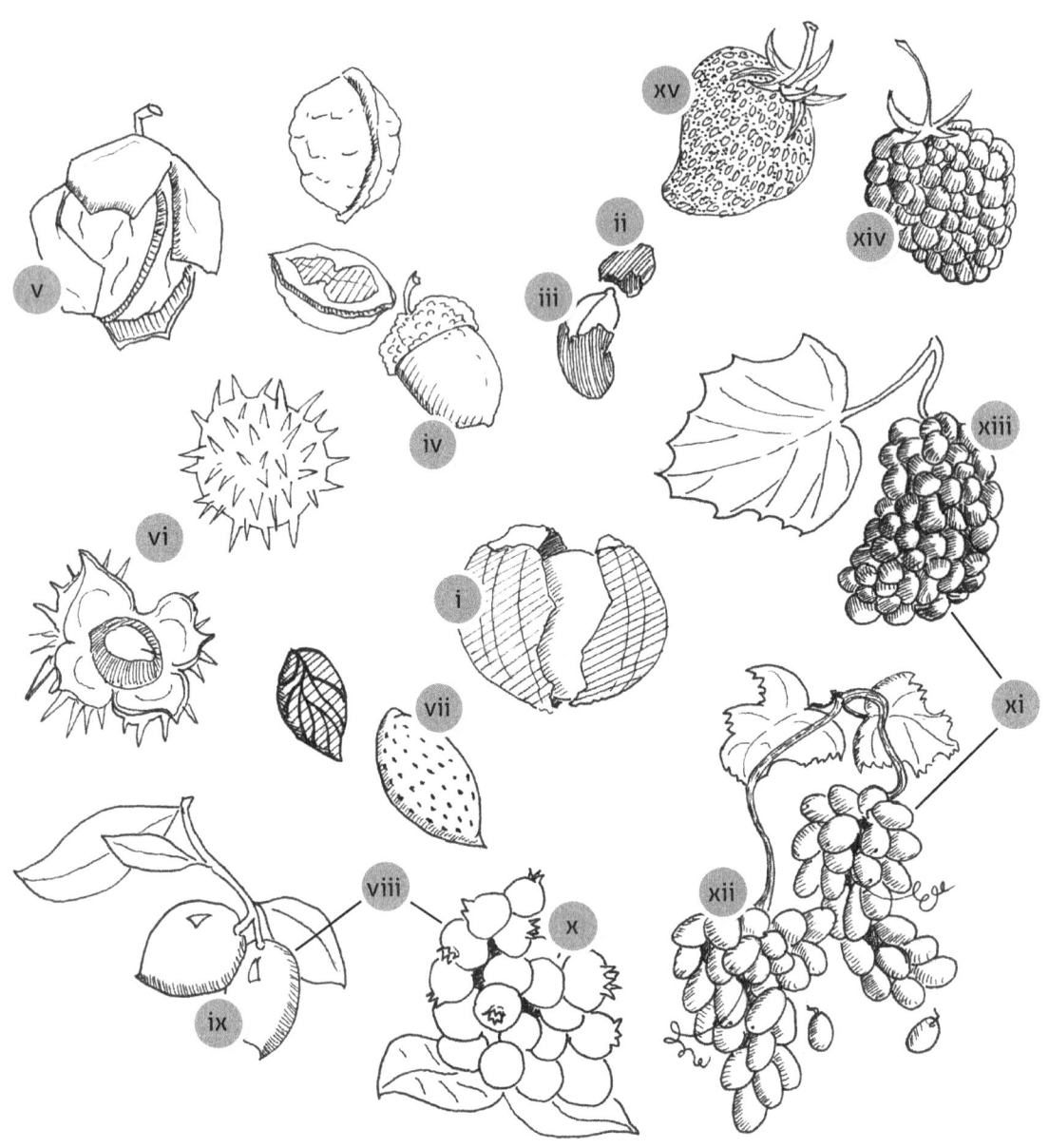

CH. 17 WORD LIST

i. putāmen, putāminis, n.
ii. cortex, corticis, m.
iii. nūcleus, -ī, m.
iv. glans, glandis, f.
v. iūglans, iūglandis, f.
vi. castanea, -ae, f.
vii. amygdalum, -ī, n.
viii. bāca, -ae, f.
ix. olea, -ae, f.
x. vaccīnium, -ī, n.
xi. acinus, -ī, m.
xii. ūva, -ae, f.
xiii. mōrum, -ī, n.
xiv. rubus, -ī, m.
xv. frāgum, -ī, n.

NUCES ET BACAE
Ch. 17

The hard outer part of a nut is called the *putāmen*, (i) inside of which is the thin *cortex*. (ii) The *cortex* encloses the *nūcleus*, (iii) which is good for food.

The oak bears the oblong *glans*, (iv) which on top is covered in a cone-shaped skin.

The walnut tree bears the wrinkled *iūglans* (v) nut, which is large and round.

The chesnut tree bears the *castanea* (vi) nut, which is enclosed in a spiny cup and is roasted for eating.

The almond tree bears the oblong *amygdalum*, (vii) which has a *putāmen* full of holes and a sweet *nūcleus*.

A small fruit that hangs down from a stem is called a *bāca*. (viii) The olive tree bears a *bāca* that is called an *olea*. (ix)

A small shrub called a *vaccīnium* (x) bears a purple *bāca* that is sweet.

A fruit that is found in a cluster is not called a *bāca*, but an *acinus*. (xi) The grapevine bears an *acinus* that is called an *ūva*. (xii)

The mulberry bush bears a purple *acinus* that is called a *mōrum*. (xiii)

The raspberry bramble bears a red or black *acinus* that is called a *rubus*. (xiv)

The strawberry plant bears a large red *acinus* that is called a *frāgum*. (xv)

Dūra exterior pars nucis appellātur *putāmen*, intrā quod est tenuis *cortex*. *Cortex* involvit *nūcleum* quī est bonus ad cibum.

Quercus fert oblongam *glandem* quae ex summā operītur triangulā cute.

Iūglans arbor fert rūgōsam *iūglandem* nucem quae est magna et rotunda.

Castanea arbor fert *castaneam* nucem quae inclūsa est echīnātō calyce et torrētur ad cibum.

Amygdala arbor fert oblongum *amygdalum* quod est *putāmine* forātō et dulcī *nūcleō*.

Parvus fructus quī dēpendet dē pediolō appellātur *bāca*. Olea arbor fert *bācam* quae appellātur *olea*.

Parva frutex appellāta *vaccīnium* fert purpuream *bācam* quae est dulcis.

Fructus quī invenītur in racēmō non appellātur *bāca*, sed *acinus*. Vītis fert *acinum* quī appellātur *ūva*.

Mōrus fert purpureum *acinum* quī appellātur *mōrum*.

Rubus fert rubrum aut nigrum *acinum* quī appellātur *rubus*.

Frāgum fert magnum rubrum *acinum* quī appellātur *frāgum*.

CH. 18 WORD LIST

i. rosa, -ae, f.
ii. līlium, -ī, n.
iii. viola, -ae, f.
iv. crocus, -ī, m.
v. rānunculus, -ī, m.
vi. chrȳsanthemum, -ī, n.
vii. narcissus, -ī, m.
viii. taraxacum,* -ī, n.
ix. myosōta, -ae, f.
x. bellis, bellidis, f.
xi. hēlianthes, hēlianthis, n.
xii. trifolium, -ī, n.
xiii. carduus, -ī, m.
xiv. tulipa,* -ae, f.
xv. hyacinthus, -ī, m.

GENERA FLORUM
Ch. 18

The red *rosa* (i) has a thorny stem.

The white *līlium* (ii) has a drooping neck and lips that curve back.

The fragrant *viola* (iii) has a purple, yellow, or white flower with heart-shaped petals.

The yellow *crocus* (iv) bears saffron useful in food and perfume.

The small *rānunculus* (v) has a slender stem and a golden or milky white flower.

The pale *chrȳsanthemum* (vi) does not wilt.

The slender *narcissus* (vii) is named after a boy who fell in love with his own reflection.

The yellow *taraxacum* (viii) sends its seeds to the wind.

The blue *myosōta* (ix) has petals which have the shape of a mouse ear.

The eye-shaped *bellis* (x) has a white flower that is yellow in the middle and red at the tips.

The giant *hēlianthes* (xi) turns itself toward the sun.

The tiny *trifolium* (xii) has a white flower and three leaves (but occasionally four).

The prickly *carduus* (xiii) has a round flower.

The pretty *tulipa* (xiv) has a flower like a cup.

The red *hyacinthus* (xv) is said to have grown where a boy once was killed by a discus.

Rubra *rosa* est spīnōsa caule.

Album *līlium* est languidō collō et labrīs resupīnīs.

Frāgrantī *violae* est purpureus, lūteus, aut albus flōs cum cordiformibus foliīs.

Lūteus *crocus* fert crocum ūtile ad cibum et unguentum.

Parvus *rānunculus* est gracilī caule et aureō aut lacteō flōre.

Subalbidum *chrȳsanthemum* nōn marcescit.

Gracilis *narcissus* nominātur ab puerō quī incidit in amōrem suī speculī.

Lūteum *taraxacum* mittit semina ventō.

Caerulea *myosōta* est foliīs flōris quae habent formam mūrīnae auris.

Oculātae *bellidī* est albus flōs quī est lūteus in mediō et rubet in extrēmīs.

Ingens *hēlianthes* vertit sē adversus sōlem.

Exigium *trifolium* est albō flōre et tribus foliis (sed nonnumquam quattuor).

Spīnōsus *carduus* est rotundō flōre.

Pulchrae *tulipae* est flōs tamquam calyx.

Ruber *hyacinthus* dīcitur prōvēnisse ubi puer olim necātus est discō.

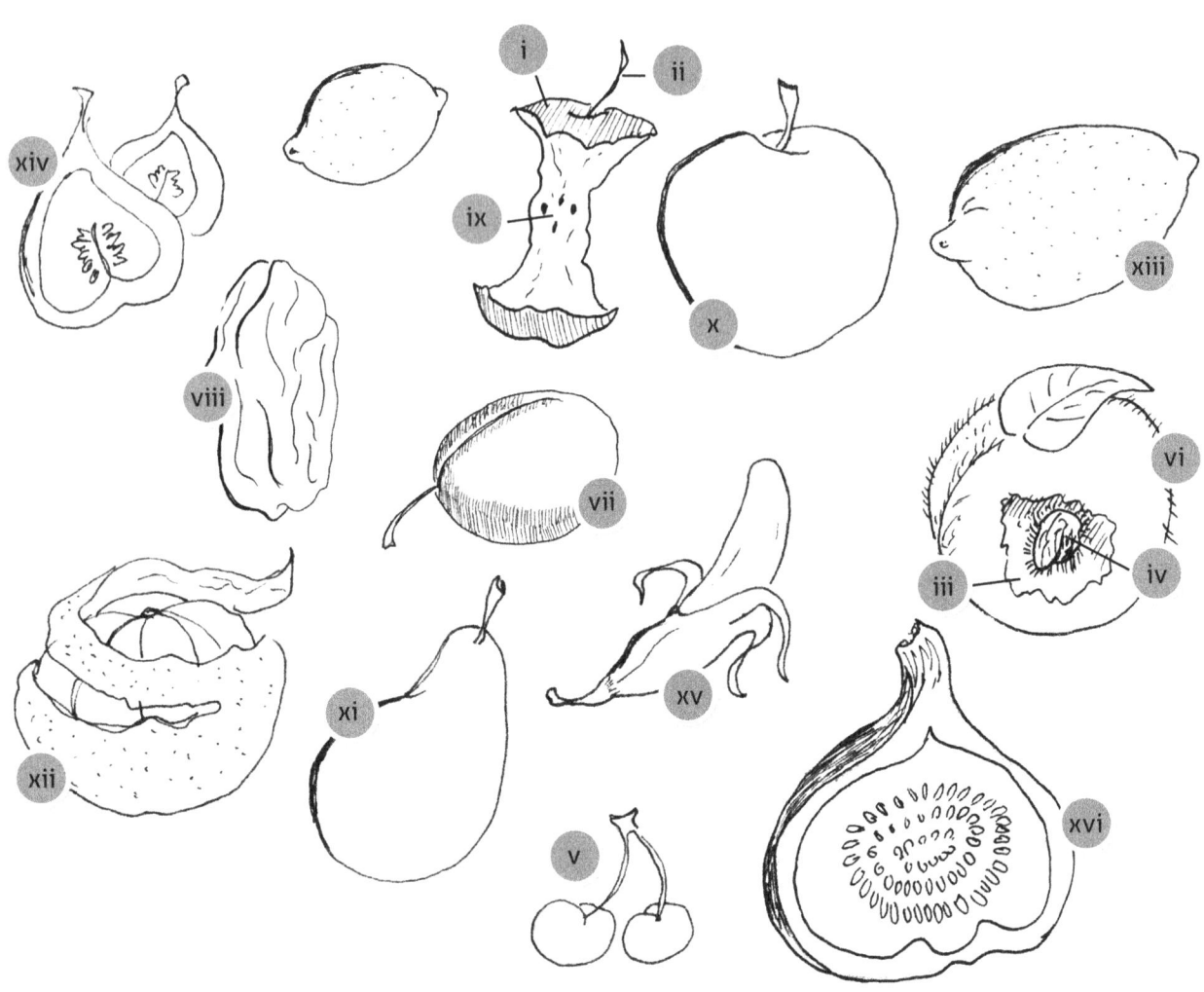

CH. 19 WORD LIST

i. cutis, -is, f.
ii. petiolus, -ī, m.
iii. pulpa, -ae, f.
iv. lignum, -ī, n.
v. cerasum, -ī, n.
vi. persicum, -ī, n.
vii. prūnum, -ī, n.
viii. palmula, -ae, f
ix. volva, -ae, f.
x. mālum, -ī, n.
xi. pirum, -ī, n.
xii. aurantium,* -ī, n.
xiii. cītreum, -ī, n.
xiv. fīcus, -ī, f.
xv. ariēna, -ae, f.
xvi. grānātum, -ī, n.

POMA

Ch. 19

A fruit is covered in *cutis* (i) and hangs down from a tree branch on a *pediolus*; (ii) inside is the *pulpa*, (iii) which people eat.

Some fruits have a round, hard seed that is called a *lignum*, (iv) such as

the red *cerasum*, (v) which hangs from a long *pediolus*;

the soft *persicum*, (vi) which is covered in fuzz;

the purple *prūnum*, (vii) which has yellow *pulpa*;

and the sweet *palmula*, (viii) which is oblong.

Some fruits have many seeds in a case that is called a *volva*, (ix) such as

the round *mālum* (x)

and the oblong *pirum*. (xi)

Some fruits have seeds throughout the *pulpa*, such as the orange *aurantium*, (xii) which has a thick *cutis*;

the sour *cītreum*, (xiii) which is either yellow or green in color;

and the brown *fīcus*, (xiv) whose tiny seeds are called grains.

The yellow *ariēna* (xv) hangs in bunches.

The *grānātum* (xvi) has berry-like fruit, which are divided by membranes.

Pōmum tegitur *cute* et pendet dē arboris rāmō in *pediolō*; intus est *pulpa* quam hominēs edunt.

Aliīs pomīs est rotundum dūrumque sēmen quod appellātur *lignum*, ut

rubrum *cerasum* quod pendet dē longō pediolō;

molle *persicum* quod tegitur lānūgine;

purpureum *prūnum* cui est lūtea *pulpa*;

et dulcis *palmula* quae est oblonga.

Alia pōma habent sēmina in tegumentō quod appellātur *volva*, ut

rotundum *mālum*

et oblongum *pirum*.

Alia pōma habent sēmina intrā *pulpam*, ut flammeum *aurantium* cui est crassa cutis;

acerbum *cītreum* quod est aut lūteum aut viride colōre;

et fusca *fīcus* cuius exigua sēmina appellantur grāna.

Lūtea *ariēna* dēpendet racēmīs.

Grānātō sunt acinī intus quī dīviduntur membrānīs.

CH. 20 WORD LIST

i. faba, -ae, f.
ii. phasēlus, -ī, m.
iii. pīsum, -ī, n.
iv. caepa, -ae, f.
v. ālium, -ī, n.
vi. rāpum, -ī, n.
vii. raphanus, -ī, m.
viii. pastināca, -ae, f.
ix. potāta,* -ae, f.
x. cucurbita, -ae, f.
xi. cucumis, cucumeris, m.
xii. pepo, peponis, m.
xiii. lycopersicum,* -ī, n.
xiv. capsicum,* -ī, n.
xv. brassica, -ae, f.
xvi. lactūca, -ae, f.
xvii. asparagus, -ī, m.
xviii. apium, -ī, n.

HOLERA ET LEGUMINA
Ch. 20

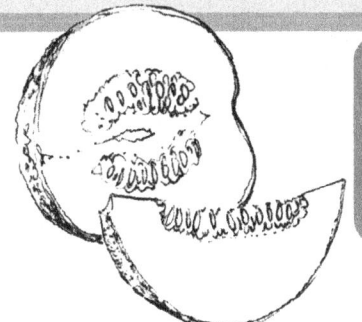

Legumes bear their fruit in pods, like
the flat-seeded *faba*, (i)
the curved-seeded *phasēlus*, (ii) and
the round-seeded *pīsum*. (iii)

In some vegetables the bulb is eaten,
such as the tearful *caepa*, (iv)
the strong-smelling *ālium*, (v)
and the purple *rāpum*. (vi)

In others the root is eaten, such as
the red *raphanus* (vii)
and the orange *pastināca*. (viii)

In others a swelling of the root is eaten, like
the brown *potāta*. (ix)

In some the fruit lies on top of the ground,
such as the hollow *cucurbita*, (x)
the green *cucumis*, (xi)
and the refreshing *pepo*. (xii)

In others the fruit hangs down from the stem,
like the juicy *lycopersicum* (xiii)
and the hot *capsicum*. (xiv)

In others the leaves themselves are eaten,
like the healthy *brassica* (xv)
and the green *lactūca*. (xvi)

In others the stem is eaten,
like the pointy *asparagus* (xvii)
and the fragrant *apium*. (xviii)

Legūmina ferunt fructum in siliquīs, ut
cui plāna sēmina sunt, *faba*;
cui curva sēmina sunt, *phasēlus*; et
cui rotunda sēmina sunt, *pīsum*.

In aliīs holeribus bulbus ēstur,
ut lacrimōsa *caepa*,
odōrum *ālium*,
et purpureum *rāpum*.

In aliīs rādix ēstur, ut
ruber *raphanus*
et flammea *pastināca*.

In aliīs tūber rādīcis ēstur, ut
fusca *potāta*.

In aliīs fructus iacet super terram,
ut inānis cucurbita,
viridis *cucumis*,
et refrīgerāns *pepo*.

In aliīs fructus dēpendet dē caule,
ut sūculentum *lycopersicum*
et fervidum *capsicum*.

In aliīs folia ipsa ēstur,
ut salūbris *brassica*
et viridis *lactūca*.

In aliīs caulis ēstur,
ut acūleātus *asparagus*
et frāgrāns *apium*.

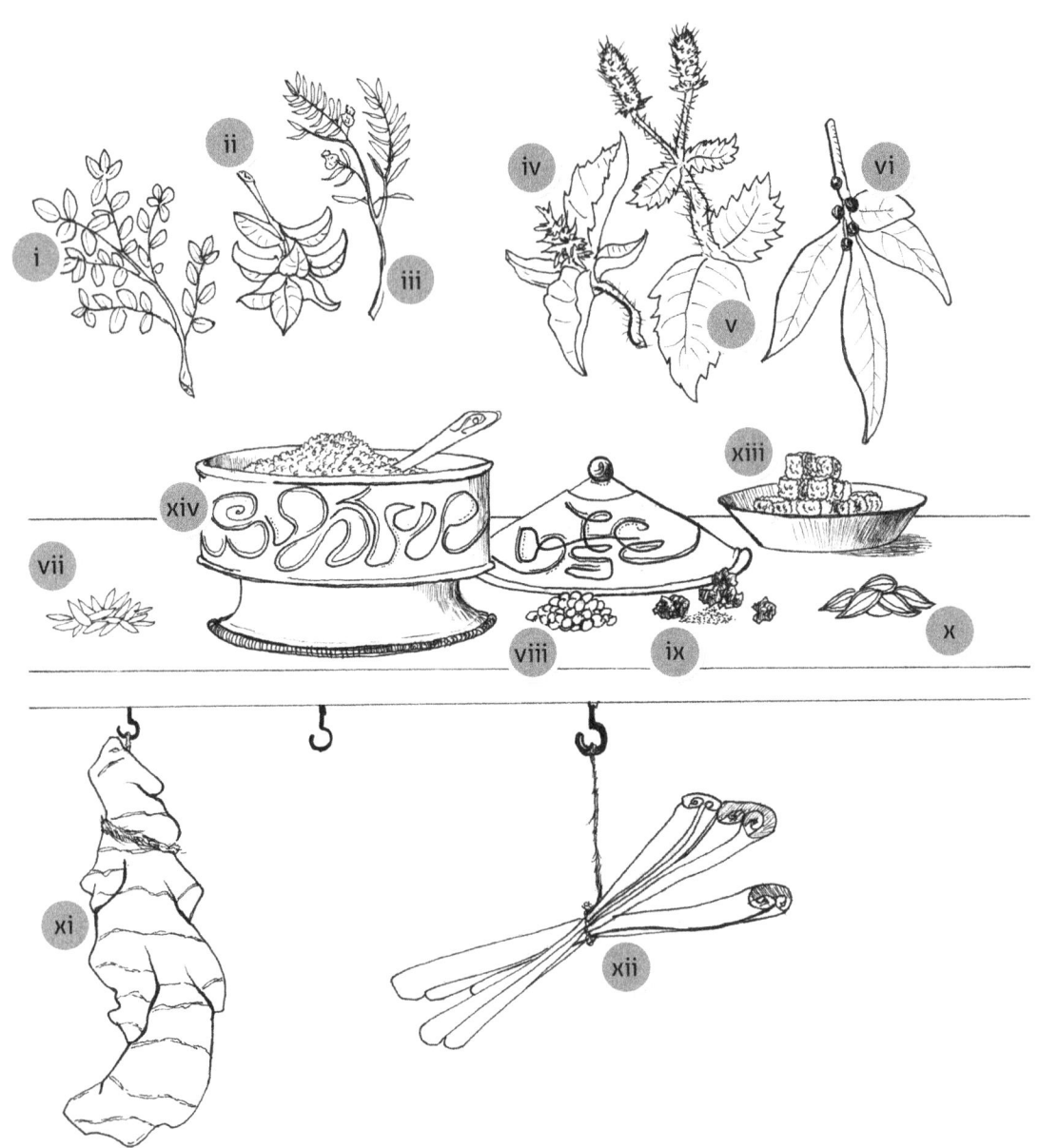

CH. 21 WORD LIST

i. thymum, -ī, n.
ii. orīganum, ī, n.
iii. rosmarīnum, -ī, n.
iv. ōcimum, -ī, n.
v. mentha, -ae, f.
vi. laurus, -ī, f.
vii. cumīnum, -ī, n.
viii. sināpis, -is, f.
ix. piper, -is, n.
x. anēthum, -ī, n.
xi. zingiber, -is, n.
xii. cinnamon, cinnamī, n.
xiii. saccharon, -ī, n.
xiv. sal, -is, f.

CONDIMENTA

Ch. 21

Some spices come from sprigs with their leaves, such as white-leaved *thymus*, (i) heat-loving *orīganum*, (ii) and sea-loving *rosmarīnum*. (iii)

Some come only from leaves, like fresh-tasting *ocīmum*, (iv) pungent-smelling *mentha*, (v) and the crown of victors, *laurus*. (vi)

Other spices come from seeds, such as long-seeded *cumīnum* (vii) yellow-seeded *sināpis* (viii) black-grained *piper*, (ix) and stomach-soothing *anēthum*. (x)

Others come from a root, such as hot *zingiber*. (xi)

Still others come from bark, such as sweet-smelling *cinnamon*. (xii)

Sweet *saccharon* (xiii) is gathered from reeds.

White *sal* (xiv) is dug from the ground.

Alia condīmenta oriuntur ex rāmulīs cum foliīs, ut cui sunt candida folia, *thymus*, quod calōrem amat, *orīganum*, et quod ad mare prōvenit, *rosmarīnum*.

Alia oriuntur sōlum ē foliīs, ut quod sapit recēns, *ocīmum*, cuius odor excitat animum, *mentha*, et corōnans victōrēs, *laurus*.

Alia condīmenta oriuntur ex sēminibus, ut quod fert oblonga sēmina, *cumīnum*, quae lutea sēmina fert, *sināpis*, cuius grāna nīgrescunt, *piper*, et quod sēdat tormina, *anēthum*.

Alia oriuntur ē rādīce, ut fervēns *zingiber*.

Alia oriuntur ex cortice, ut quod olet dulce, *cinnamon*.

Dulce *saccharon* colligitur ex harundinibus.

Alba *sal* foditur ē terrā.

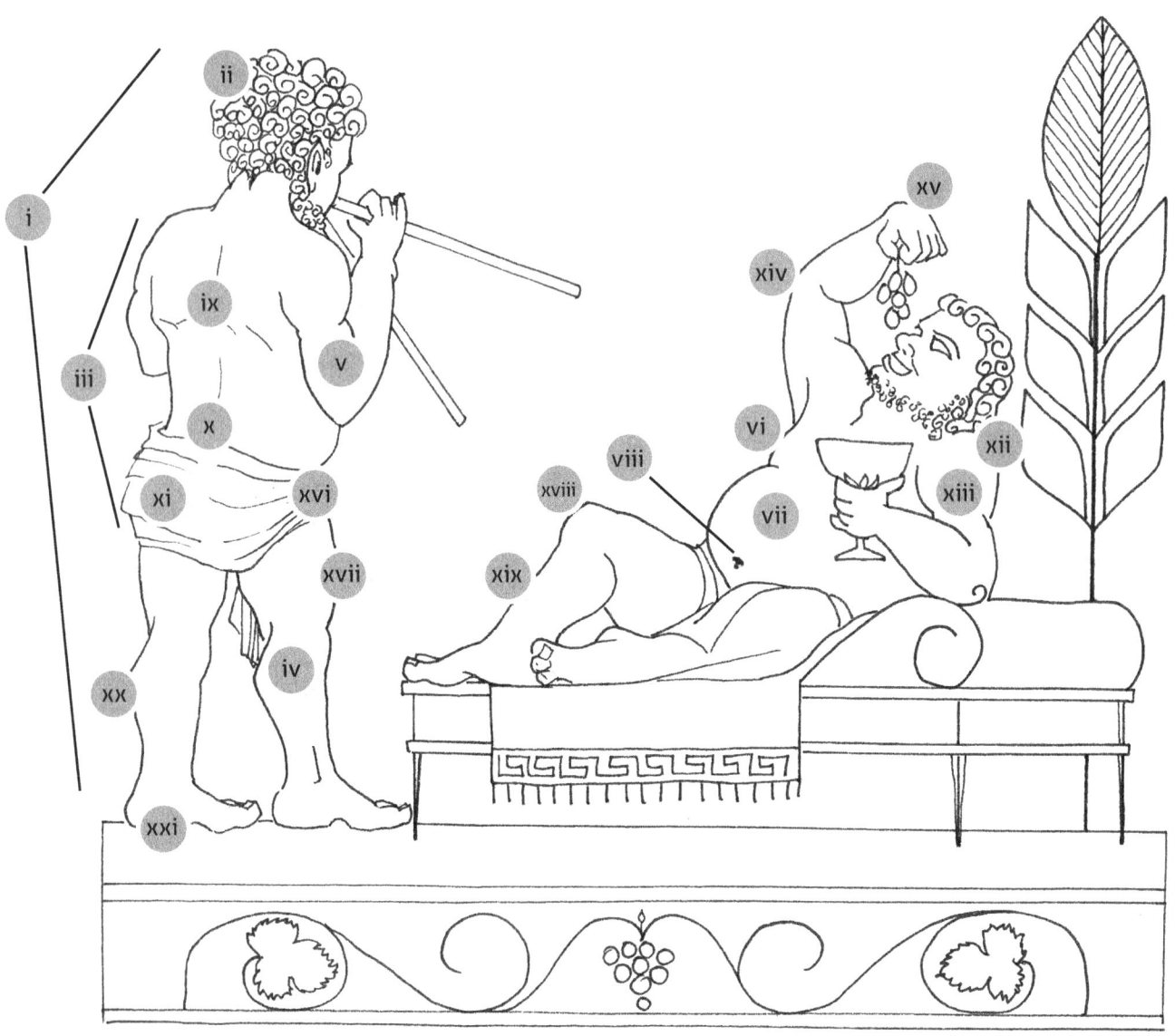

CH. 22 WORD LIST

i. corpus, corporis, n.
ii. caput, capitis, n.
iii. truncus, -ī, m.
iv. crūs, crūris, n.
v. bracchium, -ī, n.
vi. pectus, pectoris, n.
vii. alvus, -ī, f.
viii. umbīlicus, -ī, m.
ix. tergum, -ī, n.
x. lumbī, -ōrum, m. pl.
xi. natis, -is, f.
xii. umerus, -ī, m.
xiii. lacertus, -ī, m.
xiv. cubitum, -ī, n.
xv. manus, -ūs, f.
xvi. coxa, -ae, f.
xvii. femur, femoris, n.
xviii. genu, -ūs, n.
xix. tībia, -ae, f.
xx. sūra, -ae, f.
xxi. pēs, pedis, m.

CORPUS

Ch. 22

On top of the *corpus* ⓘ is the *caput*. ⓘⓘ In the middle is the *truncus*. ⓘⓘⓘ At the bottom are two limbs called *crūra*. ⓘᵥ On the sides are two limbs called *bracchia*. ᵥ

On the front side of the *truncus*, the *pectus* ᵥⓘ is above; the *alvus*, ᵥⓘⓘ below. In the middle of the *alvus* is the *umbīlicus*. ᵥⓘⓘⓘ

The rear side of the *truncus* is called the *tergum*. The lower part of the *tergum* ⓘₓ is called the *lumbī*. ₓ Below the *lumbī* are the *natēs*. ₓⓘ

At the top of the *bracchium* is a joint called the *umerus* ₓⓘⓘ that turns the entire *bracchium*.

The upper part of the *bracchium* is called the *lacertus*. ₓⓘⓘⓘ

The middle part of the *bracchium* that bends the lower *bracchium* is called the *cubitum*. ₓⓘᵥ

At the end of the *bracchium* is the *manus*, ₓᵥ which grabs and holds.

At the top of the *crūs* is a joint that is called the *coxa*. ₓᵥⓘ

The upper part of the *crūs* is called the *femur*. ₓᵥⓘⓘ

The middle part of the *crūs* that bends the lower is called the *genu*. ₓᵥⓘⓘⓘ

On the lower part of the *crūs*, in front is the *tībia* ₓⓘₓ and in the back is the *sūra*. ₓₓ

At the end of the *crūs* is the *pēs*, ₓₓⓘ which holds up the whole *corpus*.

In summō corpore est *caput*. In mediō est *truncus*. In infimō sunt duo membra appellāta *crūra*. Utrimque sunt duo membra appellāta *bracchia*.

In priōre *truncō*, *pectus* est suprā; *alvus*, infrā. In mediā *alvō* est *umbīlicus*.

Posterior *truncus* appellātur *tergum*. Inferior pars *tergī* appellātur *lumbī*. Infrā lumbōs sunt *natēs*.

In summō *bracchiō* est artus appellātus *umerus* quī vertit tōtum *bracchium*.

Superior pars *bracchiī* appellātur *lacertus*.

Media pars *bracchiī* quae flectit inferius *bracchium* appellātur *cubitum*.

In extrēmō *bracchiī* est *manus* quae prehendit et tenet.

In summō *crūre* est artus quī appellātur *coxa*.

Superior pars *crūris* appellātur *femur*.

Media pars *crūris* quae flectit inferius *crūs* appellātur *genu*.

In inferiore parte *crūris* ante est *tībia* et post est *sūra*.

In extrēmō *crūre* est *pēs* quī sustinet tōtum *corpus*.

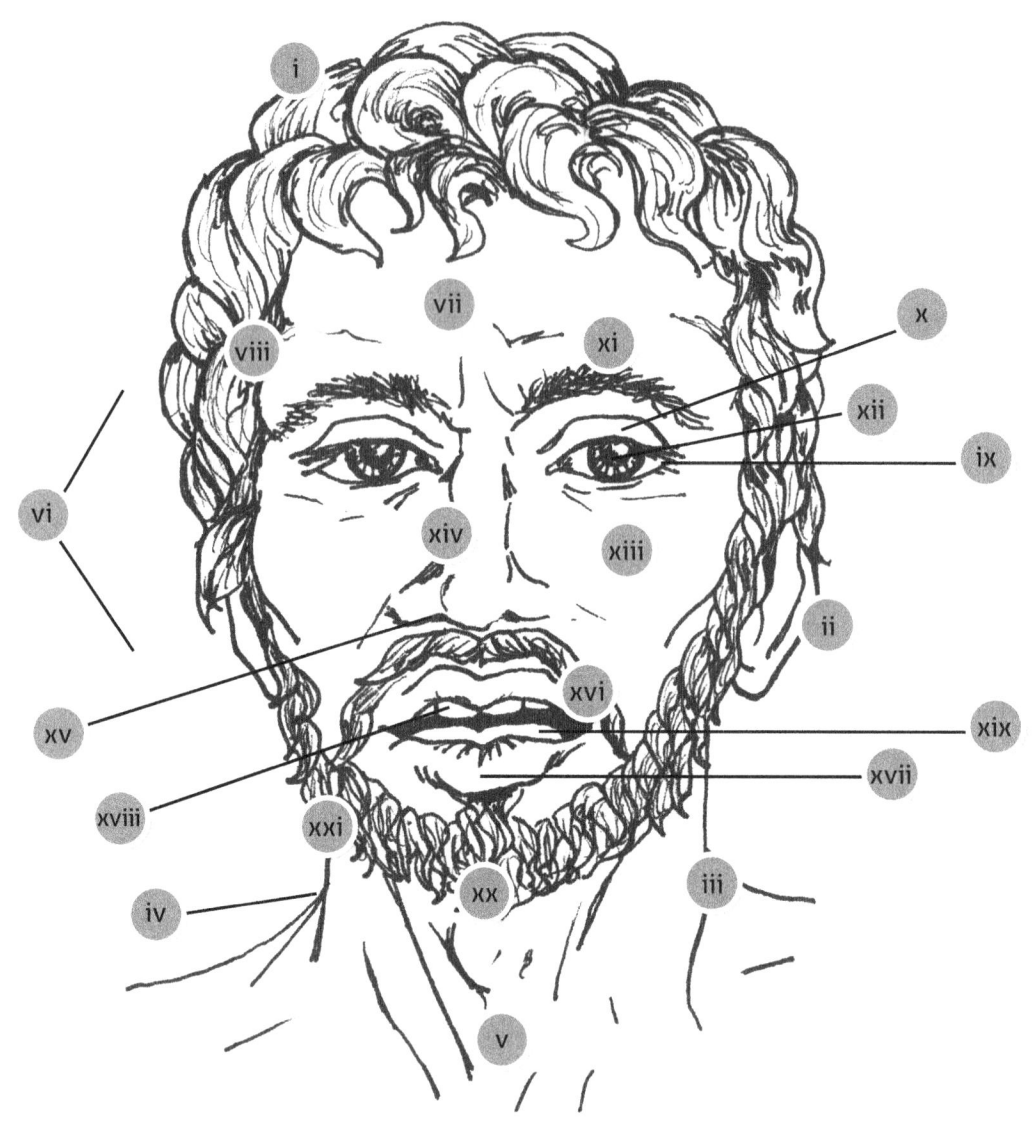

CH. 23 WORD LIST

i. capillus, -ī, m.
ii. auris, -is, f.
iii. collum, -ī, n.
iv. cervix, cervīcis, f.
v. iugulum, -ī, n.
vi. facies, -ēi, f.
vii. frons, frontis, f.
viii. tempus, temporis, n.
ix. oculus, -ī, m.
x. palpebra, -ae, f.
xi. supercilium, -ī, n.
xii. pūpilla, -ae, f.
xiii. gena, -ae, f.
xiv. nāsus, -ī, m.
xv. nāris, -is, f.
xvi. ōs, ōris, n.
xvii. lābrum, -ī, n.
xviii. dens, dentis, m.
xix. lingua, -ae, f.
xx. mentum, -ī, n.
xxi. barba, -ae, f.

CAPUT ET FACIES

Ch. 23

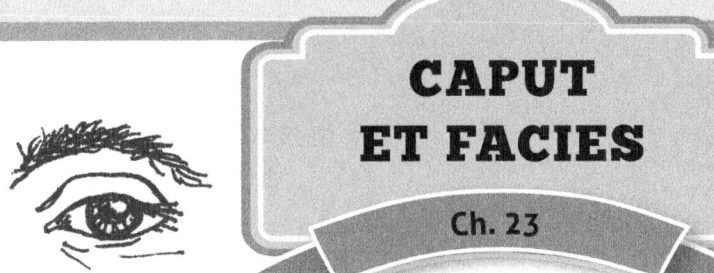

On top of the head is *capillus*. ⓘ It is black, brown, blond, or red; curly or straight.

On the sides are *aurēs*, ⓘⓘ which hear. Below, the *collum* ⓘⓘⓘ turns the head.

The back of the *collum* is called the *cervix*; ⓘᵥ the front is called the *iugulum*. ᵥ

In front is the *facies*. ᵥⓘ The highest part of the *facies*, which is below the *capillus*, is called the *frons*. On the sides, the *frons* ᵥⓘⓘ has two *tempora*. ᵥⓘⓘⓘ

Below the *frons* are two *oculī*, ⓘₓ which see, blink, and weep.

On the eye is a *palpebra* ₓ that covers it; above is a *supercilium* ₓⓘ that shades it. In the middle of the eye is the *pūpilla*. ₓⓘⓘ

Below the *oculī* are the *genae*, ₓⓘⓘⓘ which blush and pale.

Between the *oculī* is the *nāsus*. ₓⓘᵥ In the *nāsus* are openings called *nārēs*, ₓᵥ which breathe and sniff.

Below the *nāsus* is the *ōs*, ₓᵥⓘ which speaks and takes food.

The *ōs* has two *lābra*, ₓᵥⓘⓘ an upper and lower. In the *ōs* are white *dentēs* ₓᵥⓘⓘⓘ that bite and a pink *lingua* ₓⓘₓ that tastes.

Below the *ōs* is the bottom of the *facies*, which is called the *mentum*. ₓₓ

Hair on the *facies* is called *barba*. ₓₓⓘ

In summō capite est *capillus*. Est niger, fuscus, flāvus, rūfus; crispus rectusve.

Utrimque sunt *aurēs* quae audiunt. Infrā, *collum* vertit caput.

Posterius *collum* appellātur *cervix*; prius appellātur *iugulum*.

In priōrī est *facies*. Summa pars *faciēī* quae est infrā *capillum* appellātur *frons*. Utrimque *frōntī* sunt duo *tempora*.

Infrā *frontem* sunt duo *oculī* quī vident, cōnīvent, et lacrimant.

In oculō est *palpebra* quae operit eum; suprā est *supercilium* quod adumbrat eum. In mediō oculō est *pūpilla*.

Infrā oculōs sunt *genae* quae ērubescunt et pallescunt.

Inter *oculōs* est *nāsus*. In *nāsō* sunt apertūrae appellātae *nārēs* quae spīrant et olefaciunt.

Infrā *nāsum* est *ōs* quod loquītur et sūmit cibum.

Ōrī sunt duo *lābra*, superius et inferius. In ōre sunt albī *dentēs* quī mordent et rosea *lingua* quae gustat.

Infrā *ōs* est īnfima *facies* quae appellātur *mentum*.

Pilus in *faciē* appellātur *barba*.

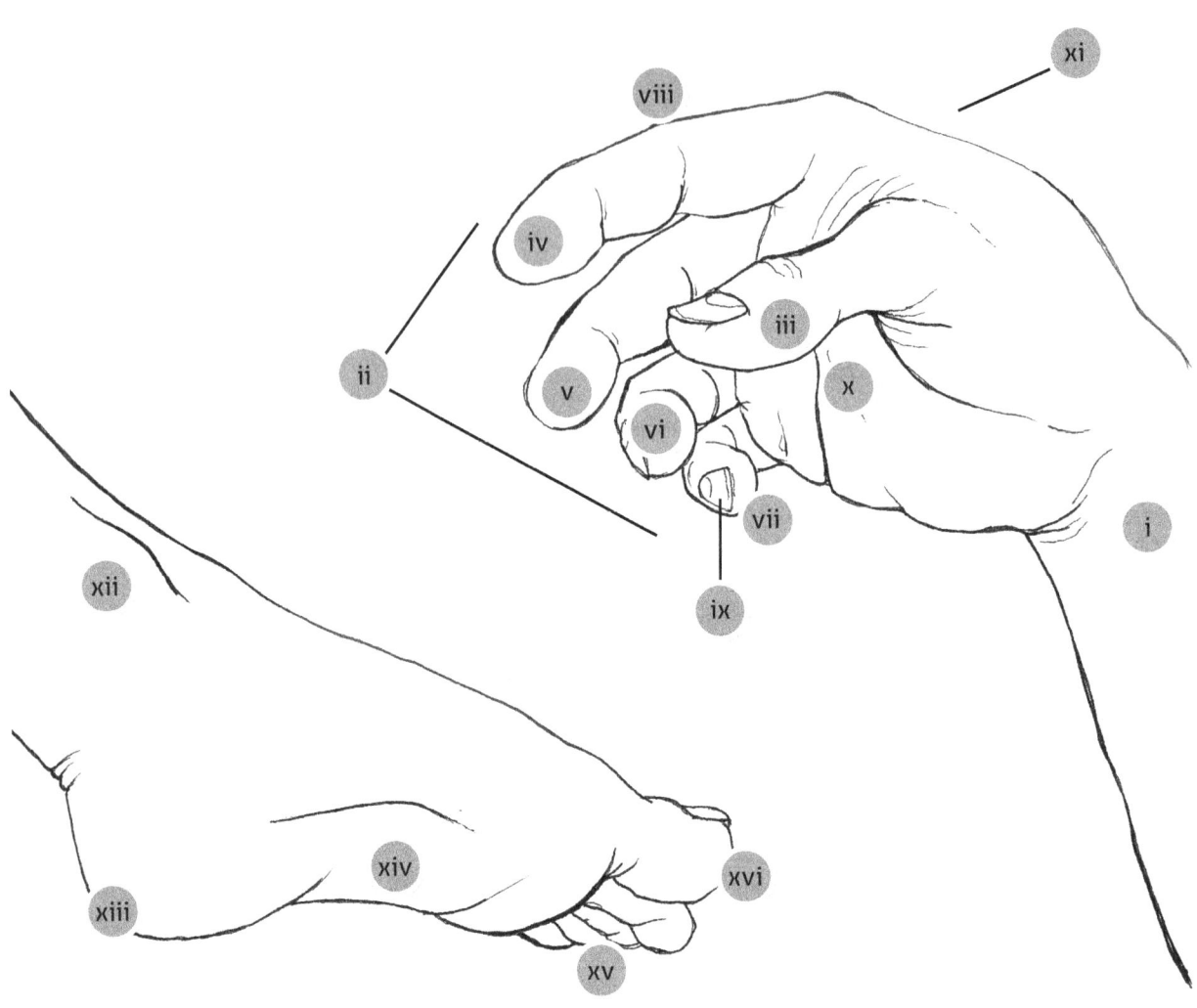

CH. 24 WORD LIST

i. carpus,* -ī, m.
ii. digitus, -ī, m.
iii. pollex, pollicis, m.
iv. index, indicis, m.
v. medius digitus, -ī, m.
vi. ānulārius digitus, -ī, m.
vii. minimus digitus, -ī, m.
viii. articulus, -ī, m.
ix. unguis, -is, f.
x. palma, -ae, f.
xi. pugnus, -ī, m.
xii. tālus, -ī, m.
xiii. calx, calcis, f.
xiv. planta, -ae, f.
xv. digitus (pedis), -ī, m.
xvi. allus, -ī, m.

MANUS ET PES
Ch. 24

The hand is joined to the arm by the *carpus*, ⓘ which turns the whole hand.

On the hand are five *digitī*. ⅱ The first and fattest is the *pollex*, ⅲ which is turned toward the others.

The second *digitus* is the *index*, ⅳ which points.

The third and longest *digitus* is the *medius*. ⅴ

The fourth *digitus* is called the *ānulārius* ⅵ and wears a ring.

The fifth *digitus* is called the *minimus* ⅶ because of the *digitī* it is the smallest.

A *digitus* has three *articulī* ⅷ which bend. At the end of the *digitus* is the hard *unguis*. ⅸ

The wide inner part of the hand is called the *palma*. ⅹ

When all five *digitī* are closed, the hand is called a *pugnus*. ⅺ

The foot is joined to the leg by the *tālus*, ⅻ which turns the whole foot.

In the back of the foot is the *calx*, ⅹⅲ which stomps and kicks.

On the bottom of the foot is the *planta*, ⅹⅳ which touches the ground.

The foot has five short and fat *digitī*. ⅹⅴ The largest is called the *allus*. ⅹⅵ

Manus adiungitur bracchiō *carpō* quī vertit tōtam manum.

In manū sunt quinque *digitī*. Primus et crassissimus est *pollex* quī vertitur adversus cēterōs.

Secundus *digitus* est *index* quī monstrat.

Tertius et longissimus *digitus* est *medius*.

Quārtus *digitus* appellātur *ānulārius* et gerit ānulum.

Quīntus *digitus* appellātur *minimus* quia ex *digitīs* est minimus.

Digitō sunt trēs *articulī* quī flectuntur. In extrēmō *digitō* est dūra *unguis*.

Lāta interior pars manūs appellātur *palma*.

Cum omnēs quinque *digitī* clauduntur *manus* appellātur *pugnus*.

Pēs adiungitur crūrī *tālō* quī vertit tōtum pedem.

In posteriōrī pede est *calx* quae calcat et calcitrat.

In inferiōrī pede est *planta* quae tangit solum.

Pedī sunt quinque brevēs et crassī *digitī*. Maximus appellātur *allus*.

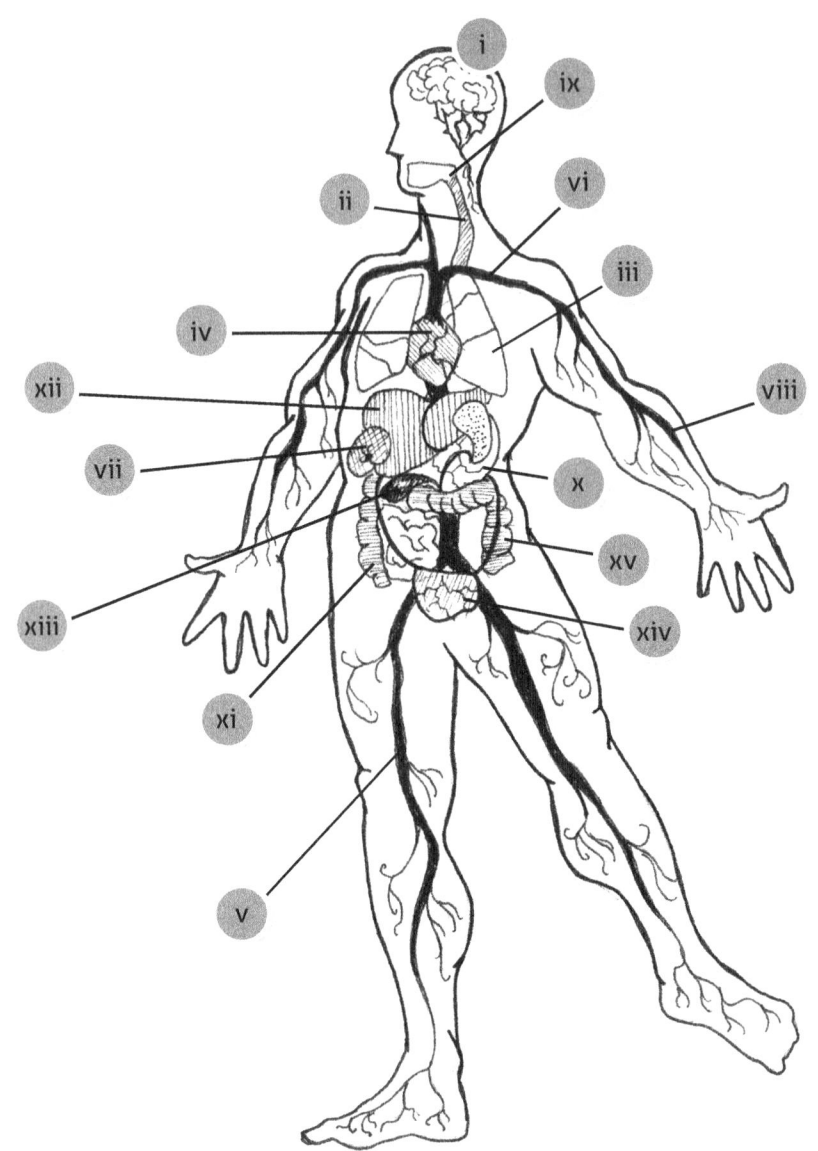

CH. 25 WORD LIST

i. cerebrum, -ī, n.
ii. trāchīa, -ae, f.
iii. pulmo, pulmōnis, m.
iv. cor, cordis, n.
v. sanguis, sanguinis, m.
vi. artēria, -ae, f.
vii. rēnēs, rēnum, m. pl.
viii. vēna, -ae, f.
ix. faucēs, faucium, f. pl.
x. venter, ventris, m.
xi. viscera, -um, n. pl.
xii. iecur, iecoris, n.
xiii. fel, fellis, n.
xiv. vēsīca, -ae, f.
xv. cōlon, -ī, n.

MEMBRA INTERIORA CORPORIS

Ch. 25

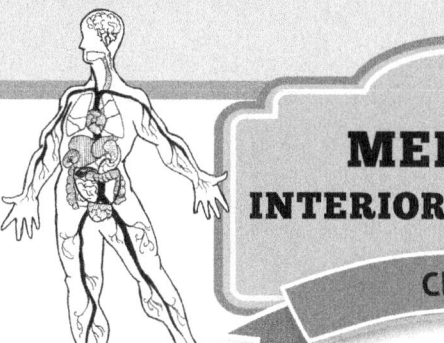

Inside the head is the *cerebrum*, (i) which guides the other parts of the body.

Breath is drawn in through the mouth or nostrils. Then it passes through the *trāchīa* (ii) into two *pulmōnēs*, (iii) and then it is pushed back out the same way.

Inside the chest is the *cor*, (iv) which beats and moves *sanguis*. (v)

Sanguis flows through *artēriae* (vi) to all the parts of the body.

The *sanguis* is filtered by two *rēnae*. (vii)

The *sanguis* returns to the *cor* through *vēnae*. (viii)

Food is chewed with the teeth and swallowed with the tongue; then it passes through the *faucēs* (ix) to the *venter* (x) where it is digested.

Then the food passes through the *viscera*. (xi)

The useful part of the food is absorbed into the *sanguis* with the help of the *iecur* (xii) and the *fel*, (xiii) and thus feeds the body.

What is left is gathered into liquid urine in the *vēsīca* (xiv) or solid excrement in the *cōlon*, (xv) which then are expelled from the body.

Intrā caput est *cerebrum* quod regit cētera membra corporis.

Anima dūcitur per ōs aut nārēs. Deinde trānsit per *trāchīam* in duōs *pulmōnēs*, et deinde expellitur eādem.

Intrā pectus est *cor* quod palpitat et movet *sanguinem*.

Sanguis fluit per *artēriās* ad omnia membra corporis.

Sanguis colātur duabus *renīs*.

Sanguis redit ad *cor* per *vēnās*.

Cibus mandūcātur dentibus et vorātur linguā; deinde trānsit per *faucēs* in *ventrem* ubi concoquitur.

Deinde cibus trānsit per *viscera*.

Pars ūtilis cibī absorbētur in *sanguinem* auxiliō *iecoris* et *fellis*, et ita alit corpus.

Reliquum colligitur in liquidum lōtium in *vēsīcā* aut solidum stercus in *cōlō*, quae deinde redduntur ex corpore.

62 · ORBIS PICTUS

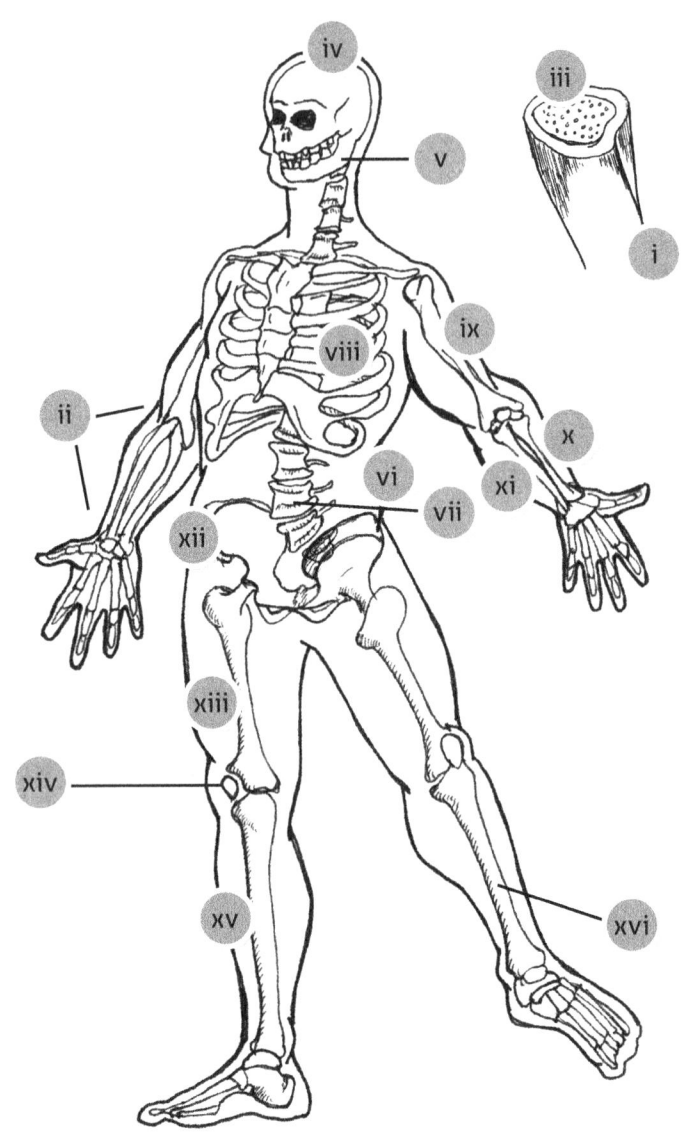

CH. 26 WORD LIST

i. os, ossis, n.
ii. artus, -ūs, m.
iii. medulla, -ae, f.
iv. calvāria, -ae, f.
v. maxilla, -ae, f.
vi. spīna, -ae, f.

vii. vertebra, -ae, f.
viii. costa, -ae, f.
ix. umerus, -ī, m.
x. radius, -ī, m.
xi. ulna, -ae, f.

xii. coxa, -ae, f.
xiii. femur, femoris, n.
xiv. patella, -ae, f.
xv. tībia, -ae, f.
xvi. fībula, -ae, f.

OSSA

Ch. 26

The shape of the body is maintained by 206 hard and white *ossa*. (i)	Fōrma corporis sustinētur ducentīs sēx dūrīs et albīs *ossibus*.
The *ossa* are joined together by *artūs*. (ii)	*Ossa* coniunguntur *artibus*.
Inside an *os* is *medulla*. (iii)	In *osse* est *medulla*.
The large and round *os* inside the *caput* is called the *calvārium*. (iv)	Magnum et rotundum *os* intrā *caput* appellātur *calvārium*.
The moveable *os* under the *calvārium* that forms the chin is called the *maxilla*. (v)	Mōbile *os* sub *calvāriō* quod facit mentum appellātur *maxilla*.
Along the middle of the back extends the *spīna*, (vi) which is made of many moveable *vertebrae*. (vii)	Per medium tergum extenditur *spīna* quae cōnstat ex multīs mōbilibus *vertebrīs*.
The twenty-four curving *ossa* that surround the chest are called the *costae*. (viii)	Vigintī quattuor curva *ossa* quae amplectuntur pectus appellantur *costae*.
Inside the arm is the *umerus* (ix) above the *cubitum;* below are the *radius* (x) and *ulna*. (xi)	Intrā bracchium est *umerus* suprā *cubitum;* infrā sunt *radius* et *ulna*.
The two large and flat *ossa* at the top of the leg are called *coxae*. (xii)	Duo magna et plāna *ossa* in summō crūre appellantur *coxae*.
The largest *os* in the body is the *femur*, (xiii) which extends from the *coxa* to the knee.	Maximum *os* in corpore est *femur* quod extenditur dē *coxā* ad genu.
A small round *os* on top the knee is called the *patella*. (xiv)	Parvum et rotundum *os* super genu appellātur *patella*.
Below the knee is the strongest *os*, the *tībia*. (xv)	Infrā genu est robūstissimum *os*, *tībia*.
The *tībia* is joined to the foot by a small *os* whose name is *fībula*. (xvi)	*Tībia* adiungitur pedī parvō *osse* cui nōmen est *fībula*.

CH. 27 WORD LIST

i. mons, montis, m.
ii. culmen, culminis, n.
iii. rūpes, rupis, f.
iv. iugum, -ī, n.
v. collis, -is, m.
vi. vallis, -is, f.
vii. convallis, -is, f.
viii. plānities, -ēī, f.
ix. fons, fontis, m.
x. rīvus, -ī, m.
xi. flūmen, fluminis, n.
xii. rīpa, -ae, f.
xiii. mare, -is, n.
xiv. ōs, ōris, n.
xv. cataracta, -ae, f.
xvi. stagnum, -ī, n.
xvii. palus, palūdis, f.

TERRA

Ch. 27

Land that reaches high into the *caelum* is called a *mons*. (i)

The very top of a *mons* is called the *culmen*. (ii)

Very steep places on a *mons* are called *rūpēs*. (iii)

A line of *montēs* is called a *iugum*. (iv)

A small *mons* is called a *collis*. (v)

Between the high *montēs* are low *vallēs*. (vi)
A deep *vallis* is called a *convallis*. (vii)

A flat place is called a *plānitiēs*. (viii)

Water bubbles out from a *fons*, (ix) and, flowing down a *mons*, makes a small *rīvus*. (x)

Many *rīvī* join together in a *vallis* and make a *flūmen*. (xi)

On each side a *flūmen* has a *rīpa*. (xii)

A *flūmen* winds itself to the *mare*. (xiii)

When the *flūmen* reaches the *mare*, it is called the *ōs* (xiv) of the *flūmen*.

When a *rīvus* or *flūmen* suddenly falls from a higher place, it is called a *cataracta*. (xv)

If a place where water collects and does not flow is small, it is called a *lacūna*; if it is larger, a *stagnum*; (xvi) if it is very large, a *lacus*.

A very wet place full of trees or grasses is called a *palus*. (xvii)

Terra quae extenditur altē in *caelum* appellātur *mons*.

Summus *mons* appellātur *culmen*.

Locī valdē arduī in *monte* appellantur *rūpēs*.

Ordo *montium* appellātur *iugum*.

Parvus *mons* appellātur *collis*.

Inter altōs *montēs* sunt humilēs *vallēs*.
Alta *vallis* appellātur *convallis*.

Plānus locus appellātur *plānitiēs*.

Aqua scatet ex *fonte* et fluēns dē *monte* facit parvum *rīvum*.

Multī *rīvī* coniunguntur in *valle* et faciunt *flūmen*.

Utrimque *flūminī* est *rīpa*.

Flūmen sinuat sē ad *mare*.

Cum *flūmen* pervenit ad *mare*, appellātur *ōs flūminis*.

Cum *rīvus* vel *flūmen* subitō praecipitat dē locō altiōre, appellātur *cataracta*.

Sī locus ubi aqua colligitur neque fluit est parvus, appellātur *lacūna*; sī māior, *stagnum*; sī ingēns, *lacus*.

Humidissima terra plēna arborum aut grāminum appellātur *palus*.

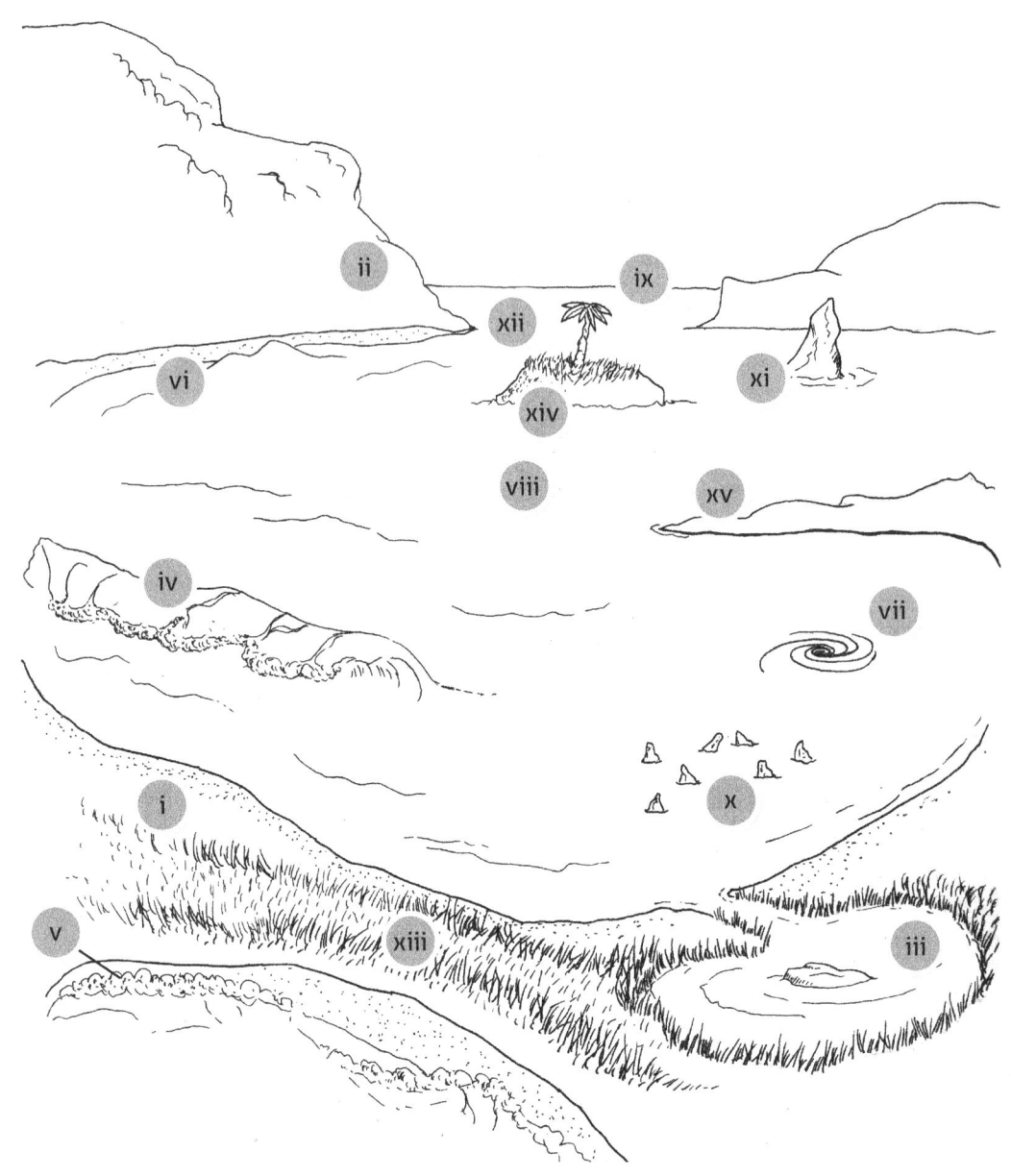

CH. 28 WORD LIST

i. lītus, lītoris, n.
ii. prōmonturium, -ī, n.
iii. sinus, -ūs, m.
iv. fluctus, -ūs, m.
v. spūma, -ae, f.
vi. aestus, -ūs, m.
vii. vorāgo, voraginis, f.
viii. aequor, -is, n.
ix. altum, -ī, n.
x. vadum, -ī, n.
xi. scopulus, -ī, m.
xii. fretum, -ī, n.
xiii. isthmus, -ī, m.
xiv. insula, -ae, f.
xv. paeninsula, -ae, f.

MARE

Ch. 28

Land meets the sea at the *lītus*. (i)

Land jutting into the sea is called a *prōmonturium*. (ii)

A place where the shoreline gives way to the sea is called a *sinus*. (iii)

Water rolling towards the shore is called a *fluctus*. (iv)

When a *fluctus* crashes, it makes white bubbles called *spūma*. (v)

With the movement of the moon, the *aestus* (vi) comes in and goes out.

Water that swirls and submerges ships is called a *vorāgo*. (vii)

The flat *mare* when it is undisturbed by the wind is called the *aequor*. (viii)

Deep sea is called the *altum*. (ix)
Shallow sea is called the *vadum*. (x)

A rock that juts out of the *mare* is called a *scopulus*. (xi)

A narrow sea between two lands is called a *fretum*. (xii)

A narrow land between two seas is called an *isthmus*. (xiii)

Land that is surrounded by sea on all sides is called an *insula*. (xiv)

Land that is almost surrounded by sea is called a *paeninsula*. (xv)

Terra attingit mare in *lītore*.

Terra ēminēns in mare appellātur *prōmonturium*.

Locus ubi ōra maritima cēdit marī appellātur *sinus*.

Aqua volvēns adversus lītus appellātur *fluctus*.

Cum fluctus pulsātur, facit albās bullās quae appellantur *spūma*.

Mōtū lūnae
aestus accēdit et recēdit.

Aqua quae circumacta mergit nāvēs appellātur *vorāgo*.

Plānum *mare* cum nōn commovētur ventō appellātur *aequor*.

Altum mare appellātur *altum*.
Vadum mare appellātur *vadum*.

Saxum quod ēminet ex marī appellātur *scopulus*.

Angustum mare inter duās terrās appellātur *fretum*.

Angusta terra inter duo maria appellātur *isthmus*.

Terra quae circumdatur marī undique appellātur *insula*.

Terra quae prope circumdatur marī appellātur *paeninsula*.

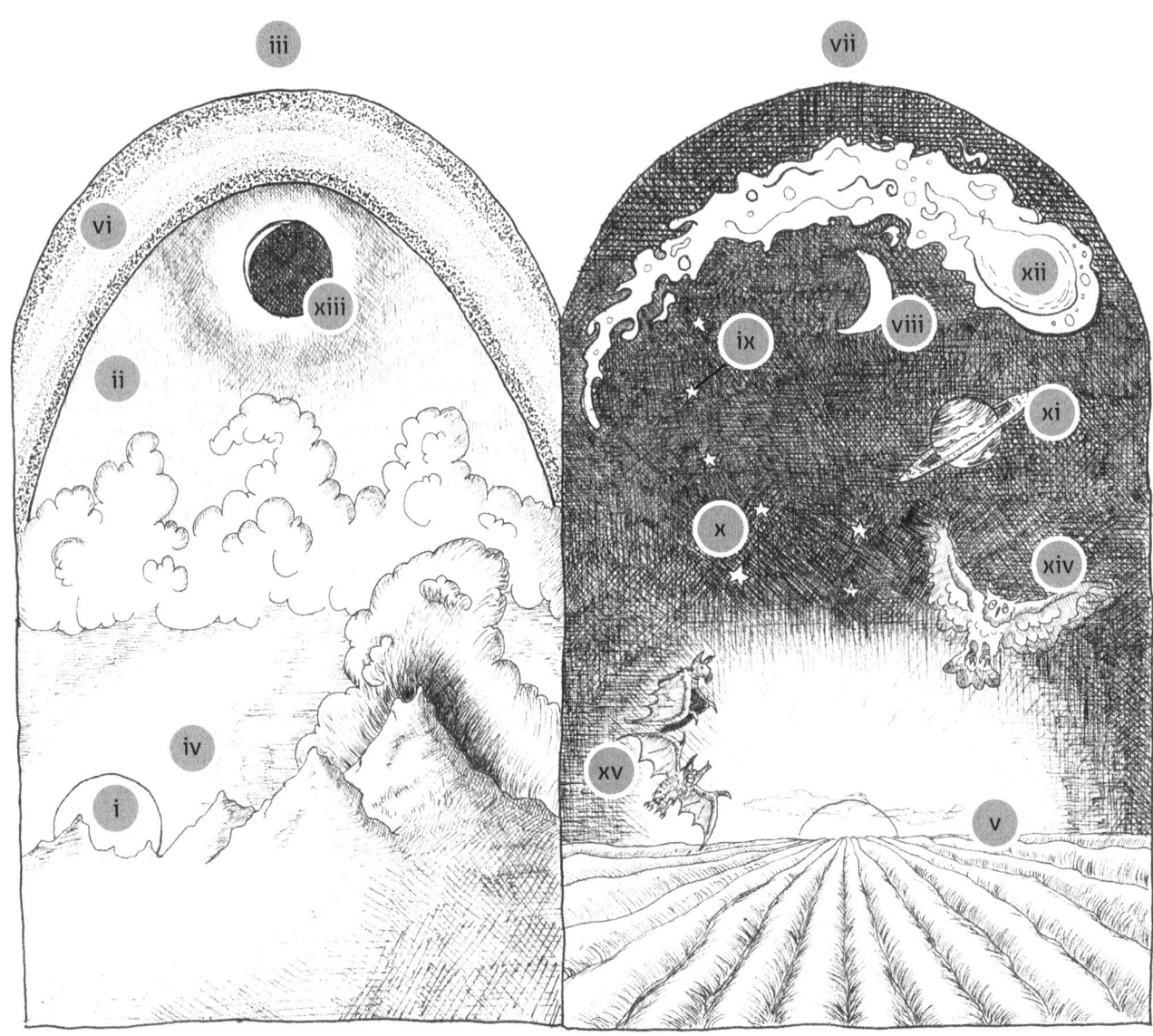

CH. 29 WORD LIST

i. sōl, sōlis, m.
ii. caelum, -ī, n.
iii. diēs, -ēī, m./f.
iv. aurōra, -ae, f.
v. crepusculum, -ī, n.
vi. īris, īridis, f.
vii. nox, noctis, f.
viii. lūna, -ae, f.
ix. stella, -ae, f.
x. constellātio, constellātiōnis, f.
xi. planēta, -ae, f.
xii. comētēs, -ae, f.
xiii. eclīpsis, -is, f.
xiv. noctua, -ae, f.
xv. vespertīlio, vespertīliōnis, f.

DIES ET NOX

Ch. 29

When the *sōl* (i) shines in the *caelum*, (ii) it is *dies*. (iii)

In the morning, when the *sōl* rises, its first light is called *aurōra*. (iv)

In the evening, when the *sōl* sets, its last light is called *crepusculum*. (v)

After rain, the many-colored *īris* (vi) sometimes appears.

After the *sōl* has set, it is *nox*. (vii)

During the *nox*, the greatest light is the *lūna*, (viii) which waxes and wanes, is full and new, crescent and gibbous.

The whole *caelum* is full of *stellae*, (ix) which twinkle and make up *constellātiōnēs*. (x)

A wandering *stēlla* is called a *planēta*. (xi)

A long-tailed *stēlla* is called a *comētēs*. (xii)

When the sun is darked by the *lūna*, it is called an *eclīpsis* (xiii) of the *sōl* or *sōlāris eclīpsis*. Likewise, when the *lūna* is darkened by the shadow of the earth, it is called an *eclīpsis* of the *lūna* or *lūnāris eclīpsis*.

During the *nox*, the *noctua* (xiv) hunts mice and the *vespertīlio*, (xv) flying insects.

Cum *sōl* lūcet in *caelō* est *dies*.

Mane cum *sōl* oritur eius prīma lux appellātur *aurōra*.

Vesperī cum sōl occidit eius ultima lux appellātur *crepusculum*.

Post imbrem multicoloris *īris* interdum appāret.

Postquam *sōl* occidit est *nox*.

Nocte maximum lūmināre est *lūna* quae augētur et minuitur, est plēna et nova, cornūta et gibbera.

Tōtum *caelum* est plēnum *stēllārum* quae micant et faciunt *constellātiōnēs*.

Errāns *stēlla* appellātur *planēta*.

Crināta *stēlla* appellātur *comētēs*.

Cum sōl obscūrātur *lūnā* appellātur *eclīpsis sōlis* vel *sōlāris eclīpsis*. Item, cum *lūna* obscūrātur umbrā terrae, appellātur *eclīpsis lūnae* vel *lūnāris eclīpsis*.

Nocte noctua venātur mūrēs, et *vespertīlio*, volāntēs bestiolās.

70 · ORBIS PICTUS

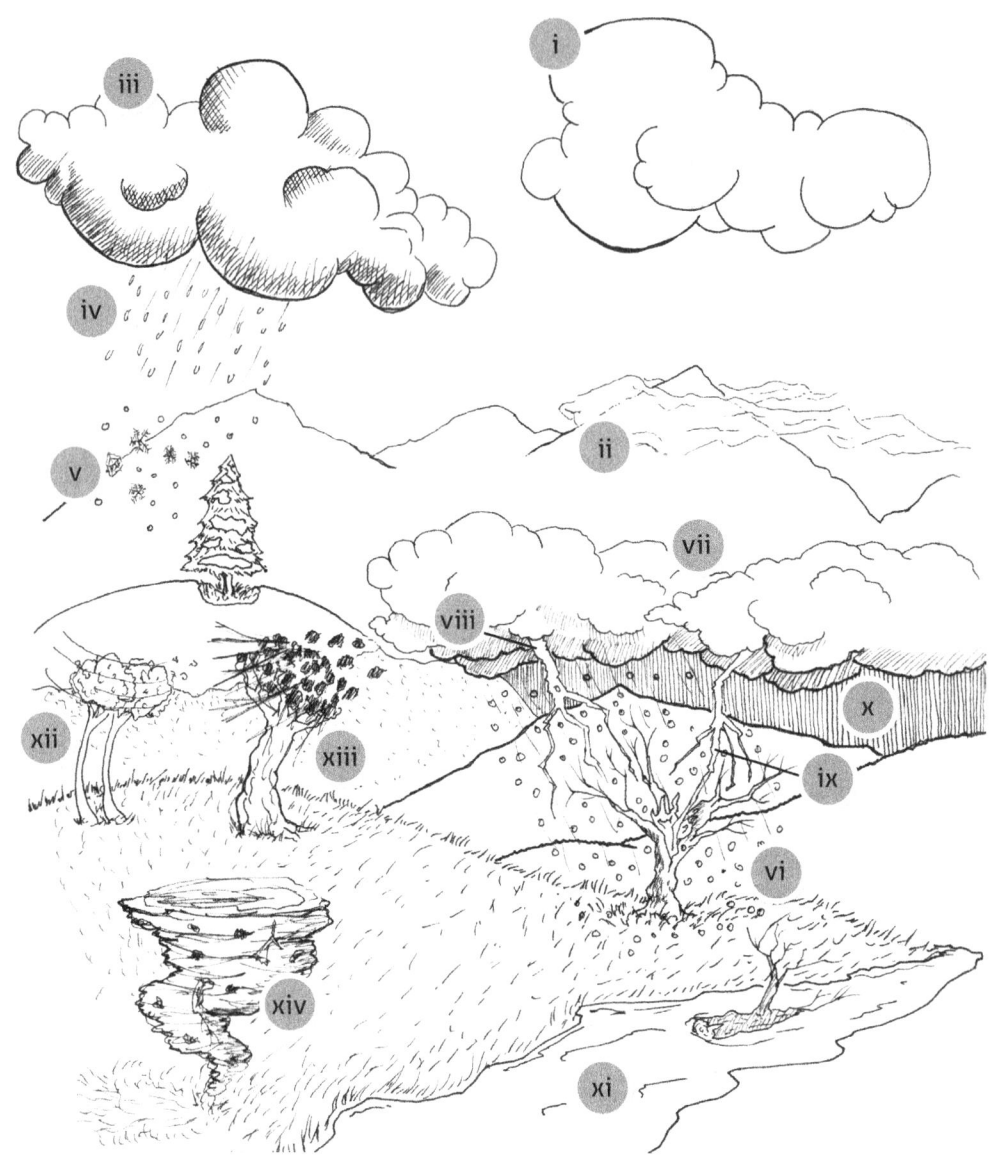

CH. 30 WORD LIST

i. nūbes, -is, f.
ii. cālīgo, cālīginis, f.
iii. nimbus, -ī, m.
iv. imber, imbris, m.
v. nix, nivis, f.
vi. grando, grandinis, f.
vii. tempestas, tempestātis, f.
viii. fulgur, -is, n.
ix. fulmen, fulminis, n.
x. tonitrus, -ūs, m.
xi. dīluvium, -ī, n.
xii. aura, -ae, f.
xiii. procella, -ae, f.
xiv. turbo, turbinis, m.

TEMPESTAS CAELI
Ch. 30

When the sky is cloudy, it is covered in white *nūbēs*. [i]

When a *nūbes* drops to the ground, it is called *cālīgo*. [ii]

When a *nūbes* brings rain, it is called a *nimbus*. [iii]

The *nimbī* pour out wet *imber*, [iv] which waters crops and feeds rivers.

In the winter, *nimbī* pour out cold, white *nix*, [v] which covers the land.

Sometimes, *nimbī* pour out hard, icy *grando*, [vi] which destroys crops.

When *nūbēs* turn dark and the wind blows strong, a *tempestas* [vii] is rising.

The sky lights up with *fulgur*, [viii] trees are struck by *fulmen*, [ix] and the ground itself shakes when the *tonitrus* [x] booms.

Rivers swollen with too much *imber* run over their banks, and both people and animals are swept away by a *dīluvium*. [xi]

A wind that blows gently is called an *aura*. [xii]

A wind that blows very strong is called a *procella*. [xiii]

A wind that whirls around and circles one place is called a *turbo*. [xiv]

Cum caelum est nūbilum operītur albīs *nūbibus*.

Cum *nūbes* dēscendit ad terram appellātur *cālīgo*.

Cum *nūbes* affert imbrem appellātur *nimbus*.

Nimbī effundunt ūmidum *imbrem* quī rigat frūgēs et alit fluviōs.

Hieme *nimbī* effundunt frīgidam et albam *nivem* quae operit terram.

Interdum *nimbī* effundunt dūrum et gelātum *grandinem* quī perdit frūgēs.

Cum *nūbēs* fiunt atrae et ventus flat validē *tempestas* orītur.

Caelum illustrātur *fulgure*, arborēs iciuntur *fulmine*, et terra ipsa quatitur cum *tonitrus* sonat.

Flūmina tumida nimiō *imbre* trānseunt rīpās, et hominēs et bestiae dēferuntur *dīluviō*.

Ventus quī flat lentē appellātur *aura*.

Ventus quī flat validissimē appellātur *procella*.

Ventus quī circumagitur et ambit ūnum locum appellātur *turbo*.

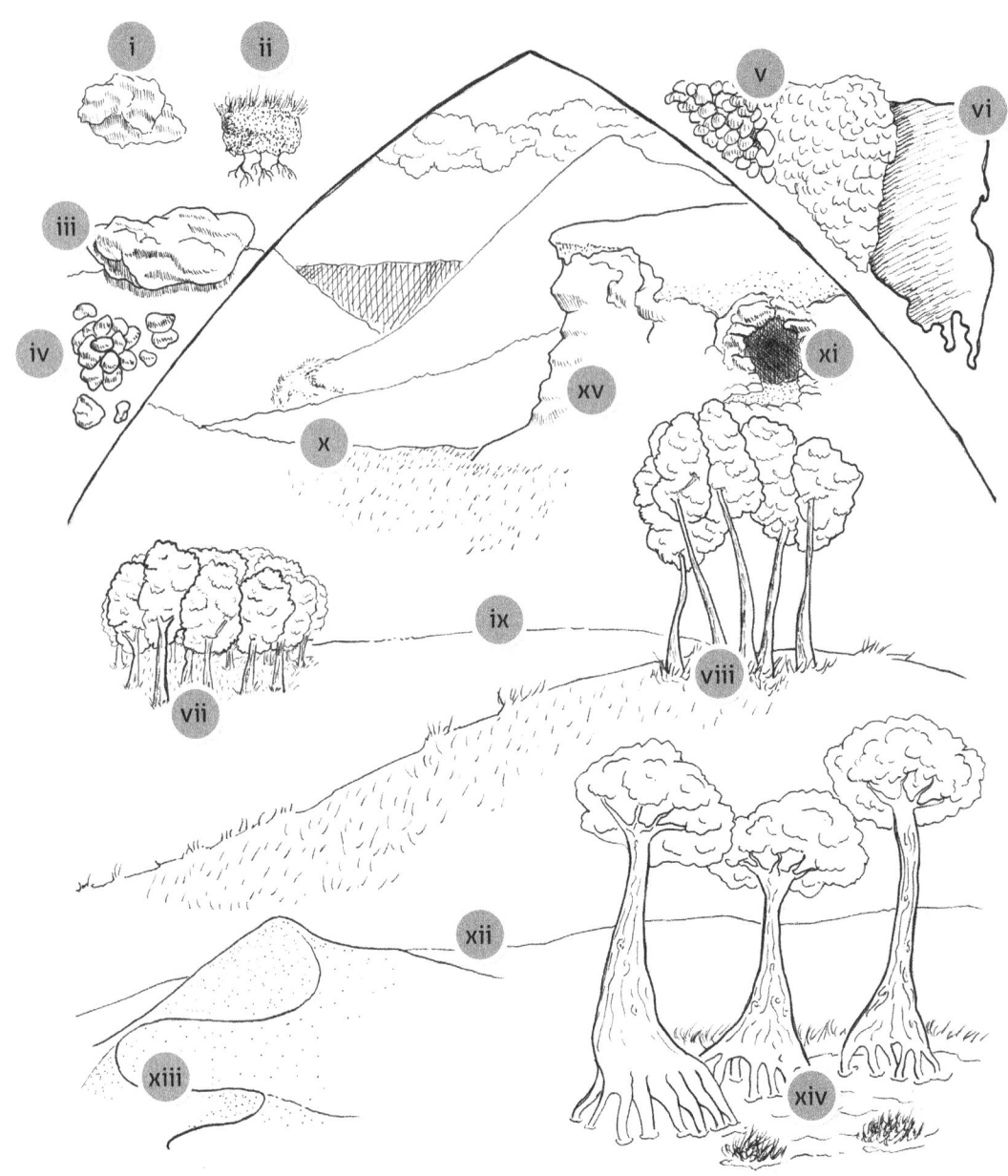

CH. 31 WORD LIST

i. glaeba, -ae, f.
ii. caespes, caespitis, m.
iii. saxum, -ī, n.
iv. lapis, lapidis, m.
v. sabulo, sabulōnis, m.
vi. līmus, -ī, m.
vii. silva, -ae, f.
viii. lūcus, -ī, m.
ix. campus, -ī, m.
x. prātum, -ī, n.
xi. antrum, -ī, n.
xii. sōlitūdo, sōlitūdinis, f.
xiii. harēnae, -ārum, f. pl.
xiv. palus, palūdis, f.
xv. rūpes, -is, f.

GENERA TERRAE
Ch. 31

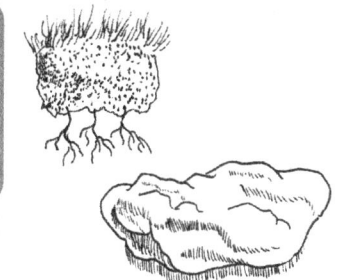

A lump of earth is called a *glaeba*.	Massa terrae appellātur *glaeba*.
A *glaeba* with grass is also called *caespes*.	*Glaeba* cum grāmine etiam appellātur *caespes*.
A hardened lump of earth is called a *saxum*.	Dūrāta massa terrae appellātur *saxum*.
A small *saxum* is called a *lapis*.	Parvum *saxum* appellātur *lapis*.
Earth full of *lapidēs* is called *sabulo*.	Terra plēna *lapidum* appellātur *sabulo*.
Wet earth is called *līmus*.	Hūmida terra appellātur *līmus*.
A place with trees is called a *silva*.	Locus cum arboribus appellātur *silva*.
A small *silva* is called a *lūcus*.	Parva *silva* appellātur *lūcus*.
An open, flat place is a *campus*.	Apertus et aequus locus est *campus*.
A grassy *campus* is called a *prātum*.	Herbōsus *campus* appellātur *prātum*.
A hollowed out *saxum* is an *antrum*.	Cavum *saxum* est *antrum*.
A vast place where no one lives is called a *sōlitūdo*.	Vastus locus ubi nēmō habitat appellātur *sōlitūdo*.
A dry *sōlitūdo* without trees or plants is called a *harēnae*, where the earth is full of tiny grains.	Sicca *sōlitūdo* sine arboribus aut stirpibus appellātur *harēnae* ubi terra est plēna exiguōrum grānōrum.
A wet place is called a *palus*.	Hūmidus locus appellātur *palus*.
A very steep *saxum* is called a *rūpes*.	Arduum *saxum* appellātur *rūpes*.

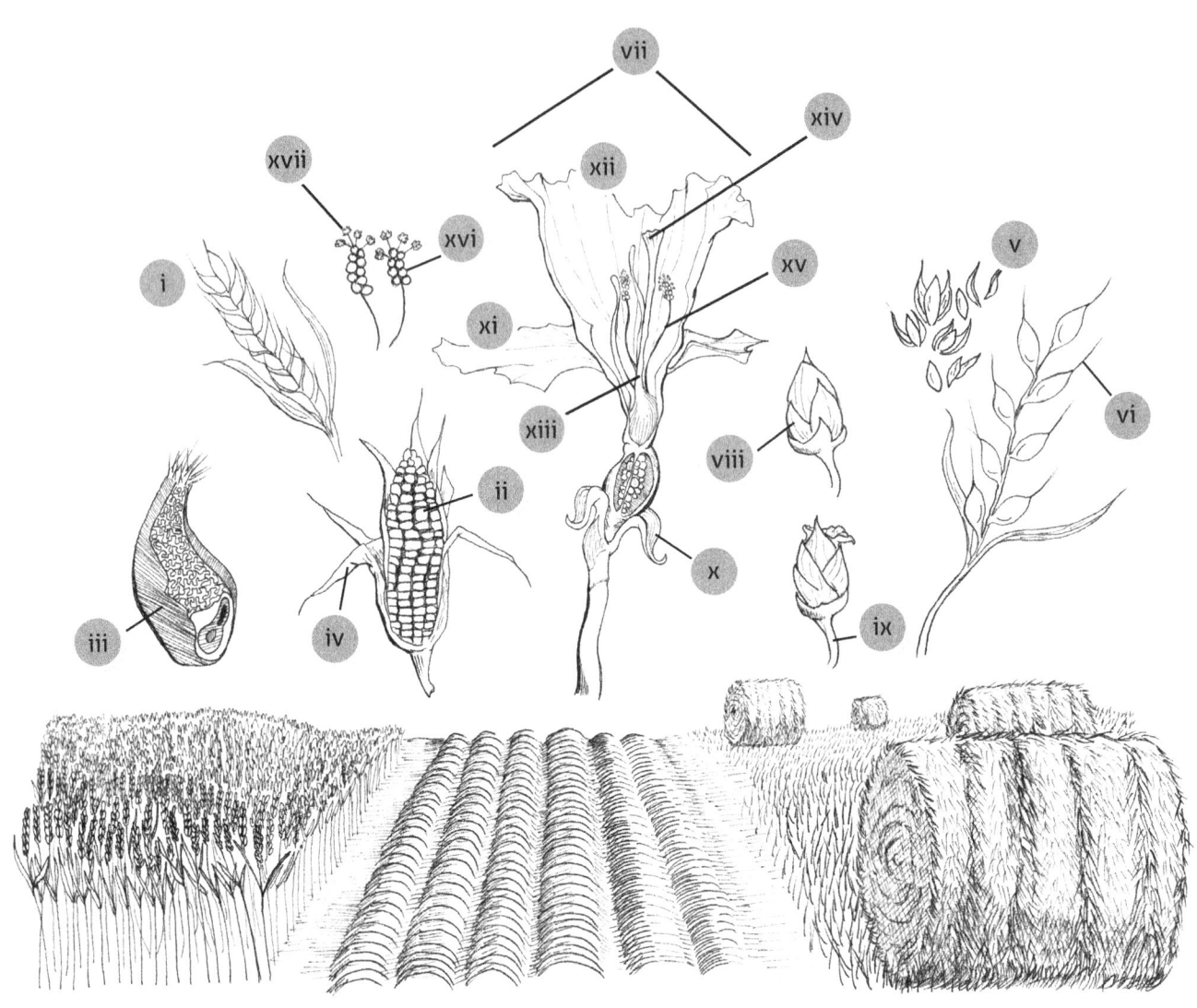

CH. 32 WORD LIST

i. spīca, -ae, f.
ii. grānum, -ī, n.
iii. furfur, -is, m.
iv. glūma, -ae, f.
v. palea, -ae, f.
vi. arista, -ae, f.
vii. flōs, flōris, m.
viii. gemma, -ae, f.
ix. caulis, -is, f.
x. calyx, calycis, m.
xi. petalium,* -ī, n.
xii. corolla,* -ae, f.
xiii. pistillum,* -ī, n.
xiv. stigma,* stigmatis, n.
xv. stāmen,* stāminis, n.
xvi. anthēra,* -ae, f.
xvii. pollen,* pollinis, n.

MEMBRA FLORIS ET FRUMENTI
Ch. 32

Grain grows as a blade of grass, and soon is topped in a *spīca*. (i)

In the *spīca*, many *grāna* (ii) are enclosed, which are good for food.

The outer part of the *grānum*, which is hard and dark, is called *furfur*. (iii)

The *grānum* itself is enclosed in a wrapper, which is called a *glūma*. (iv) Once the *granum* is removed, the empty *glūma* is called *palea*. (v)

The thin needles that stick out of the *glūma* are called the *arista*. (vi)

Many plants and trees bear a colorful *flōs*, (vii) which attracts bees.

The *flōs* begins as a closed *gemma*, (viii) which blooms at the end of a *caulis*. (ix)

The circle of leaves at the base of the *flos* is called a *calyx* (x) or "cup."

Each of the colored leaves of the *flos* is called a *petalium*. (xi)

All of the *petalia* together are called the *corolla*, (xii) which is a word that means "little crown."

The column in the center of a *flos* is called a *pistillum*. (xiii) On top of the *pistillum* is the *stigma*. (xiv)

Each of the threads that stand around the *pistillum* is called a *stāmen*. (xv)

On top each *stāmen* is an *anthēra*, (xvi) which makes a dust called *pollen*. (xvii)

Frūmentum crescit in herbā et mox culminātur in *spīcam*.

In *spīcā* multa *grāna* inclūduntur quae sunt bona ad cibum.

Exterior pars *grānī* quae est dūra et nigra appellātur *furfur*.

Grānum ipsum inclūditur tegmine quod appellātur *glūma*. *Grānō* adēmptō *glūma* inānis appellātur *palea*.

Tenuēs acūs quī ēminent ē *glūma* appellantur *arista*.

Multae stirpēs et arborēs ferunt multicolōrem *flōrem* quī allicit apēs.

Flōs incipit in clausā *gemmā* quae florescit in extrēmā *caule*.

Circulus foliōrum in basī *flōris* appellātur *calyx* vel "pōculum."

Quodque ex colōrātīs foliīs *flōris* appellātur *petalium*.

Omnia *petalia* ūniversa appellantur *corolla* quod vocābulum significat "parva corōna."

Columna in mediō *flōre* appellātur *pistillum*. In summō pistillō est *stigma*.

Quodque fīlum quod stat circum *pistillum* appellātur *stāmen*.

In summō *stāmine* est *anthēra* quae facit farīnam appellātam *pollen*.

[This page intentionally left blank.]

GLOSSARY
Latin-English

CH. 1

WORD LIST	SINGULAR	PLURAL
i. **animal,** animālis, n., *animal*	ánimal	animália
ii. **homo,** -hominis, c., *man*	hómo	hómines
iii. **bestia,** -ae, f., *beast*	béstia	béstiae
iv. **quādrupēs,** quādrupedis, f., *quadruped*	quádrupes	quadrúpedes
v. **mammal,** mammālis, n., *mammal*	mámmal	mammália
vi. **reptile,** -is, n., *reptile*	réptile	reptília
vii. **amphibion,*** -ī, n., *amphibian*	amphíbion	amphíbia
viii. **avis,** -is, f., *bird*	ávis	áves
ix. **piscis,** -is, m., *fish*	píscis	písces
x. **bestiola,** -ae, f., *bug*	bestíola	bestíolae
xi. **insectum,** -ī, n., *insect*	inséctum	insécta
xii. **arānea,** -ī, m., *spider*	aránea	aráneae
xiii. **vermis,** -is, , *worm*	vérmis	vérmes
xiv. **pullus,** -ī, m., *chick; cub, kid, etc.*	púllus	púlli
xv. **catulus,** -ī, m., *cub, kid, kitten, etc.*	cátulus	cátuli

SYNONYMS
avis: āles, ālitis, m./f.; volucris, -is, f.
bestia: fera, -ae, f.

CH. 2

WORD LIST	SINGULAR	PLURAL
i. **pilus,** -ī, m., *hair*	pílus	píli
ii. **villus,** -ī, m., *fur*	víllus	vílli
iii. **lāna,** -ae, f., *wool*	lána	-----
iv. **saeta,** -ae, f., *bristle, whisker*	saéta	saétae
v. **iuba,** -ae, f., *mane*	iúba	iúbae

WORD LIST	SINGULAR	PLURAL
vi. **acūleus,** -ī, m., *quill*	acúleus	acúlei
vii. **cutis,** -is, f., *skin*	cútis	cútes
viii. **pellis,** -is, f., *hide*	péllis	pélles
ix. **corium,** -ī, n., *leathery hide*	córium	cória
x. **testa,** -ae, f., *shell*	tésta	testae
xi. **cornū,** -ūs, n., *horn*	córnu	córnua
xii. **dens,** dentis, m., *tusk*	déns	déntes
xiii. **unguis,** -is, f., *nail, claw, talon*	únguis	úngues
xiv. **ungula,** -ae, f., *hoof*	úngula	úngulae

EXTRA
floccus, -ī, m., *tuft of wool*
vellus, velleris, n., *fleece*

SYNONYMS
acūleus: spīna, -ae, f.
floccus: mallus, -ī, m.
pellis: tergus, tergoris, n.
testa: cortex, corticis, m.; crusta, -ae, f.; putāmen, putāminis, n.

CH. 3

WORD LIST	SINGULAR	PLURAL
i. **branchiae,** -ārum, f. pl., *gills*	-----	bránchiae
ii. **cauda,** -ae, f., *tail*	caúda	caúdae
iii. **dorsum,** -ī, n., *back*	dórsum	dórsa
iv. **pinna,** -ae, f., *fin*	pínna	pínnae
v. **squāma,** -ae, f., *scale*	squáma	squámae
vi. **spīna,** -ae, f., *spine*	spína	spínae
vii. **āla,** -ae, f., *wing*	ála	álae
viii. **penna,** -ae, f., *feather*	pénna	pénnae
ix. **plūma,** -ae, f., *down feather*	plúma	plúmae
x. **rōstrum,** -ī, n., *beak*	róstrum	róstra
xi. **crista,** -ae, f., *crest*	crísta	crístae
xii. **ōvum,** -ī, n., *egg*	óvum	óva
xiii. **nīdus,** -ī, m., *nest*	nídus	nídi
xiv. **testa,** -ae, f., *shell*	tésta	téstae
xv. **vitellus,** -ī, m., *yolk*	vitéllus	vitélli
xvi. **albūmen,** albūminis, n., *egg white*	albúmen	albúmina

SYNONYMS

ala: pinna, -ae, f.
albumen: albumentum, -ī, n.; album -ī, n.
dorsum: tergum, -ī, n.; tergus, -oris, n.

squama: lepis, lepidis, f.
testa: putāmen, putāminis, n.; cortex, corticis, m.
vitellus: modiolum, -ī, n.

CH. 4

WORD LIST	SINGULAR	PLURAL
i. **canis,** -is, c., *dog*	cánis	cánes
ii. **fēles,** -is, f., *cat*	féles	féles
iii. **bōs,** bovis, c., *cow*	bos	bóves
iv. **vacca,** -ae, f., *female cow*	vácca	váccae
v. **taurus,** -ī, m., *bull*	taúrus	taúrī
vi. **vitulus,** -ī, m., *calf*	vítulus	vítulī
vii. **ovis,** -is, f., *sheep*	óvis	óves
viii. **ariēs,** ariētis, m., *ram*	áries	ariétes
ix. **agnus,** -ī, m., *lamb*	ágnus	ágnī
x. **hircus,** -ī, m., *billy goat, goat*	híreus	hírcī
xi. **equus,** -ī, m., *horse*	équus	équī
xii. **equulus,** -ī, m., *foal*	équulus	équulī
xiii. **asinus,** -ī, m., *donkey*	ásinus	ásinī
xiv. **sūs,** suis, c., *pig*	sús	súes
xv. **porca,** -ae, f., *sow*	pórca	pórcae
xvi. **porcellus,** -ī, m., *piglet*	porcéllus	porcéllī
xvii. **gallīna,** -ae, f., *chicken, hen*	gallína	gallínae
xviii. **gallus,** -ī, m., *rooster*	gállus	gállī
xix. **pullus gallīnāceus,** -ī, m., *chick (chicken)*	púllus gallináceus	púllī gallinácei
xx. **anas,** anatis, f., *duck*	ánas	ánates

EXTRA

anser, -is, m., *goose*
bucula, -ae, f., *young cow*
capra, -ae, f., *nanny goat*
cuniculus, -ī, m., *rabbit*
equa, -ae, f., *mare*
gallopāvo,* gallopāvōnis, m., *turkey*
haedus, -ī, m., *kid*
mulus, -ī, m., *mule*
mus, muris, c., *mouse*

porcus, -ī, m., *hog*
probata, -ōrum, n. pl., *sheep*
sucula, -ae, f., *piglet*
scrōfa, -ae, f., *breeding sow*

SYNONYMS

porcus: verres, -is, m.
porcellus: porculus, -ī, m.
hircus: caper, caprī, m.

CH. 5

WORD LIST	SINGULAR	PLURAL
i. **leo,** leōnis, m., *lion*	léo	leónes
ii. **tīgris,** -is, f., *tiger*	tígris	tígres
iii. **pardus,** -ī, m., *leopard, panther*	párdus	párdi
iv. **ursus,** -ī, m., *bear*	úrsus	úrsi
v. **lupus,** -ī, m., *wolf*	lúpus	lúpi
vi. **vulpes,** -is, f., *fox*	vúlpes	vúlpes
vii. **anguis,** -is, c., *viper*	ánguis	ángues
viii. **draco,** dracōnis, m., *python, boa*	dráco	dracónes
ix. **crocodīlus,** -ī, m., *crocodile*	crocodílus	crocodíli
x. **hyaena,** -ae, f., *hyena*	hyaéna	hyaénae
xi. **sīmia,** -ae, f., *ape, monkey*	símia	símiae
xii. **cynocephalus,** -ī, m., *baboon*	cynocéphalus	cynocéphali
xiii. **satyrus,** -ī, m., *chimpanzee*	sátyrus	sátyri
xiv. **gorilla,*** -ae, f., *gorilla*	gorílla	goríllae

EXTRA
leaena, -ae, f., *lioness*
pongo,* -ōnis, m., *orangutan*

SYNONYMS
anguis: vīpera, ae, f.; coluber, colubrī, m.; aspis, aspidis, f.
draco: pȳthon, -ōnis, m.; boa, -ae, f.
pardus: leopardus, -ī, m.; panthera, -ae, f.

CH. 6

WORD LIST	SINGULAR	PLURAL
i. **camēlus,** -ī, m., *camel*	camélus	caméli
ii. **camēlopardus,** -ī, m., *giraffe*	camelopárdus	camelopárdi
iii. **aper,** aprī, m., *boar*	áper	ápri
iv. **cervus,** -ī, m., *deer, stag*	cérvus	cérvi
v. **alcē,** -ēs, f., *elk*	álce	álces
vi. **damma,** -ae, f., *antelope*	dámma	dámmae
vii. **elephans,** elephantis, m., *elephant*	élephans	elephántes
viii. **rhīnoceros,** rhīnocerōtis, m., *rhinoceros*	rhinóceros	rhinocerótes
ix. **hippopotamus,** -ī, m., *hippopotamus*	hippopótamus	hippopótami
x. **zebra,*** -ae, f., *zebra*	zébra	zébrae
xi. **rūpicapra,** -ae, f., *mountain goat*	rupícapra	rupícaprae
xii. **strūthio,** strūthiōnis, m., *ostrich*	strúthio	struthiónes

EXTRA
bison, bisontis, m., *buffalo*
camēla, -ae, f., *female camel*

SYNONYMS
aper: verres, -is, m.
camēlopardus: camēlopardalis, -is, f.
hippopotamus: equus fluviātilis, -is, m.
rhīnoceros: ūnicornis, -is, m.; asinus Indicus, -ī, m.
strūthio: strūthiocamēlus, -ī, m.

CH. 7

WORD LIST	SINGULAR	PLURAL
i. **lepus,** leporis, m., *hare*	lépus	lépores
ii. **mūs,** mūris, m., *mouse, rat*	mus	múres
iii. **sciūrus,** -ī, m., *squirrel*	sciúrus	sciúri
iv. **cunīculus,** -ī, m., *rabbit, coney*	cunículus	cunículi
v. **talpa,** -ae, f., *mole*	tálpa	tálpae
vi. **fiber,** fibrī, m., *beaver*	fíber	fíbri
vii. **lūtra,** -ae, f., *otter*	lútra	lútrae
viii. **ērināceus,** -ī, m., *hedgehog*	erináceus	erinácei
ix. **hystrix,** hystricis, f., *porcupine*	hýstrix	hýstrices
x. **mustēla,** -ae, f., *weasel*	mustéla	mustélae
xi. **procyon,*** procyōnis, m., *raccoon*	prócyon	procyónes
xii. **mēles,** -is, f., *badger*	méles	méles
xiii. **testūdo,** testūdinis, f., *turtle*	testúdo	testúdines
xiv. **rāna,** -ae, f., *frog*	rána	ránae
xv. **lacerta,** -ae, f., *lizard*	lacérta	lacértae

EXTRA
būfo, bufōnis, m., *toad*
chamaeleon, chamaeleōnis, m., *chameleon,*
  lit. *"color-changing lizard"*
ichneumon, -is, m., *mongoose*
mus maximus, -ī, m., *rat*
cunīculum, -ī, n., *burrow*
salamandra, -ae, f., *salamander*

stellio, stelliōnis, m., *newt, stellion*
testūdo terrestris, -is, f., *tortoise*
vespertīlio, vespertīliōnis, m., *bat*
viverra, -ae, f., *ferret*

SYNONYMS
fiber: castor, -is, m.
testūdo: chelys, f.

CH. 8

WORD LIST	SINGULAR	PLURAL
i. **aquila,** -ae, f., *eagle*	áquila	áquilae
ii. **milvus,** -ī, f., *kite*	mílvus	mílvi
iii. **accipiter,** accipitris, m., *hawk*	accípiter	accípitres
iv. **falco,** falcōnis, m., *falcon*	fálco	falcónes
v. **vultur,** vulturis, m., *vulture*	vúltur	vúltures
vi. **būteo,** būteōnis, m., *buzzard*	búteo	buteónes
vii. **cornix,** cornīcis, f., *crow*	córnix	corníces
viii. **corvus,** -ī, m., *raven*	córvus	córvi
ix. **būbo,** būbōnis, m., *any horned owl*	búbo	bubónes
x. **strix,** strigis, f., *any earless owl*	strix	stríges
xi. **tytō,*** tytois, f., *any barn owl*	týto	týtoes

EXTRA

noctua, -ae, f., *any night owl*

SYNONYMS

accipiter: būteo, būteōnis, m.
būbo: ōtus, -ī, m.
strix; tytō: ulula, -ae, f.

CH. 9

WORD LIST	SINGULAR	PLURAL
i. **cygnus,** -ī, m., *swan*	cýgnus	cýgni
ii. **anas,** anatis, f., *duck*	ánas	ánates
iii. **anser,** anseris, m., *goose*	ánser	ánseres
iv. **grus,** gruis, f., *crane*	grús	grúes
v. **ardea,** -ae, f., *heron, bittern*	árdea	árdeae
vi. **phoenīcopterus,** -ī, m., *flamingo*	phoenicópterus	phoenicópteri
vii. **cicōnia,** -ae, f., *stork*	cicónia	cicóniae
viii. **pelicānus,** -ī, m., *pelican*	pelicánus	pelicáni
ix. **gavia,** -ae, f., *seagull*	gávia	gáviae
x. **haliaetus,** -ī, m., *osprey, sea eagle*	haliaétus	haliaétī
xi. **diomedēa,*** -ae, f., *albatross*	diomedéa	diomedéae

SYNONYMS

cygnus: olor, olōris, m.
gavia: larus, -ī, m.
pelicānus: onōcrotalus, -ī, m.

CH. 10

WORD LIST	SINGULAR	PLURAL
i. **rubecula,*** -ae, f., *red robin*	rubécula	rubéculae
ii. **luscinia,** -ae, f., *nightingale*	luscínia	luscíniae
iii. **passer,** -is, m., *sparrow*	pásser	pásseres
iv. **columba,** -ae, f., *dove*	colúmba	colúmbae
v. **palumba,** -ae, f., *pigeon*	palúmba	palúmbae
vi. **pīcus,** -ī, m., *woodpecker*	pícus	píci
vii. **psittacus,** -ī, m., *parrot*	psíttacus	psíttaci
viii. **pāvo,** pavōnis, m., *peacock*	pávo	pavónes
ix. **cōturnix,** coturnicis, f., *quail*	cotúrnix	cotúrnices
x. **tetrao,** tetraōnis, m., *grouse*	tétrao	tetraónes
xi. **phāsiāna,** -ae, f., *pheasant*	phasiána	phasiánae
xii. **gallopāvo,*** gallopāvōnis, m., *turkey*	gallopávo	gallopavónes

EXTRA
canaria,* -ae, f., *canary*
merula, -ae, f., *blackbird*
turdus, -ī, m., *thrush*

SYNONYMS
coturnix: ortygia, -ae, f.
rubecula: erithacus, -ī, m.; turdus, -ī, m.

CH. 11

WORD LIST	SINGULAR	PLURAL
i. **bālaena,** -ae, f., *whale*	baláena	baláenae
ii. **cētus,** -ī, m., *sperm whale*	cétus	céti
iii. **delphīnus,** -ī, m., *dolphin*	delphínus	delphíni
iv. **phōca,** -ae, f., *seal, sea lion, walrus*	phóca	phócae
v. **squalus,** -ī, m., *shark*	squálus	squáli
vi. **pōlypus,** -ī, m., *octopus*	pólypus	pólypi
vii. **sēpia,** -ae, f., *squid*	sépia	sépiae
viii. **urtīca,** -ae, f., *jellyfish*	úrtica	úrticae
ix. **lōcusta,** -ae, f., *lobster*	locústa	locústae
x. **cancer,** cancrī, m., *crab*	cáncer	cáncri
xi. **concha,** -ae, f., *shellfish, clam*	cóncha	cónchae

EXTRA
chēle, -ēs, f., *claw*
crusta, -ae, f., *thin shell, exoskeleton*
cōrālium, -ī, n., *coral, esp. red coral*

echīnus, -ī, m., *sea urchin*
mūrex, mūricis, m., *purple fish*
musculus, -ī, m., *mussel*
odobēnus,* -ī, m., *walrus*

orca, -ae, f., *killer whale*
ostrea, -ae, f., *oyster*
pecten, pectinis, n., *scallop*
squilla, -ae, f., *shrimp*

SYNONYMS
bālaena: cetus, -ī, m.
concha: conchȳlium, -ī, n.

locusta: cammarus, -ī, m.
mūrex: pupura, -ae, f.
musculus: ostracium, -ī, n.
phoca: vitulus marinus, -ī, m.
polypus: octopus, -ī, m.
sēpia: lōlīgo, lōlīginis, f.
squalus: pistris, -is, f.; canis marīnus, -ī, m.

CH. 12

WORD LIST	SINGULAR	PLURAL
i. apis, -is, f., *bee*	ápis	ápes
ii. formīca, -ae, f., *ant*	formíca	formícae
iii. musca, -ae, f., *fly*	músca	múscae
iv. vespa, -ae, f., *wasp*	véspa	véspae
v. cicāda, -ae, f., *grasshopper*	cicáda	cicádae
vi. gryllus, -ī, m., *cricket*	grýllus	grýlli
vii. arānea, -ī, m., *spider*	aránea	aráneae
viii. centipeda, -ae, f., *centipede*	centípeda	centípedae
ix. libella,* -ae, f., *dragonfly*	libélla	libéllae
x. ērūca, -ae, f., *caterpillar*	erúca	erúcae
xi. lumbrīcus, -ī, m., *earthworm*	lumbrícus	lumbríci
xii. culex, culicis, m., *mosquito, gnat, midge*	cúlex	cúlices
xiii. ricinus, -ī, m., *tick*	rícinus	rícini
xiv. scarabaeus, -ī, m., *beetle*	scarabáeus	scarabáei
xv. vermīculus, -ī, m., *maggot, larva*	vermículus	vermículi
xvi. pāpilio, pāpiliōnis, m., *butterfly*	papílio	papiliónes
xvii. tinea, -ae, f., *moth*	tínea	tíneae
xviii. blatta, -ae, f., *cockroach*	blátta	bláttae

EXTRA
asīlus, -ī, m., *horsefly*
cīmex, cīmicis, m., *bedbug*
coclea, -ae, f., *snail*
crābro, crābrōnis, m., *hornet*
curculio, curculiōnis, m., *weevil*
līmax, līmācis, f., *slug*
millepeda, -ae, f., *millepede*
pedīculus, -ī, m., *louse*

pūlex, pūlicis, m., *flea*
scorpio, scorpiōnis, m., *scorpion*

SYNONYMS
apis: apicula, -ae, f. (*lit. "little bee"*)
asīlus: tabānus, -ī, m.; oestrus, -ī, m.
libella: libellula, -ae, f.
scorpio: scorpius, -ī, m.

CH. 13

WORD LIST	SINGULAR	PLURAL
i. **apis,** -is, f., *bee*	ápis	ápes
ii. **mel,** mellis, n., *honey*	mél	mélla
iii. **alvus,** -ī, f., *hive*	álvus	álvi
iv. **rēgīna,*** -ae, f., *queen*	regína	regínae
v. **acūleus,** -ī, m., *stinger*	acúleus	acúlei
vi. **lānūgo,** lānūginis, f., *fuzz*	lanúgo	-----
vii. **fūcus,** -ī, m., *drone*	fúcus	fúci
viii. **sucus,** -ī, m.,	súcus	súci
ix. **favus,** -ī, m., *comb*	fávus	fávi
x. **cēra,** -ae, f., *wax*	céra	cérae
xi. **cella,** -ae, f., *cell, compartment, room*	célla	céllae
xii. **exāmen,** exāminis, n., *swarm*	exámen	exámina

SYNONYMS
acūleus: dolō, dolōnis, m.; spīculum, -ī, n. **rēgīna:** rex, rēgis, m. [classically]

CH. 14

WORD LIST	SINGULAR	PLURAL
i. **arbor,** -is, f., *tree*	árbor	árbores
ii. **frutex,** fruticis, m., *bush, shrub*	frútex	frútices
iii. **stirps,** stirpis, f., *plant*	stirps	stírpes
iv. **vēpres,** -is, f., *briar*	vépres	vépres
v. **vītis,** -is, f., *vine*	vítis	vítes
vi. **hedera,** -ae, f., *ivy;*	hédera	héderae
vii. **harundo,** harundinis, f., *reed, cane*	harúndo	harúndines
viii. **filix,** filicis, f., *fern*	fílix	fílices
ix. **grāmen,** grāminis, n., *grass*	grámen	grámina
x. **scirpus,** -ī, m., *rush*	scírpus	scírpi
xi. **frūmentum,** -ī, n., *any type of grain*	fruméntum	fruménta
xii. **legūmen,** legūminis, n., *legume*	legúmen	legúmina
xiii. **muscus,** -ī, m., *moss*	múscus	músci
xiv. **bōlētus,** -ī, m., *mushroom*	bolétus	boléti

EXTRA
fungus, -ī, m., *fungus* **līchen,** līchēnis, m., *lichen*
herba, -ae, f., *blade of grass* **siliqua,** -ae, f., *pod*

SYNONYMS
frumentum: seges, segetis, f.
grāmen: herba, -ae, f.
harundo: calamus, -ī, m.; canna, -ae, f.
hedera: helix, helicis, f.
scirpus: iuncus, -ī, m.
stirps: caulis, -is, m.; herba,* -ae, f.; planta,*
    -ae, f.
vēpres: dūmus, -ī, m.; rubus, -ī, m.; sentis, -is, m.
vītis: lābrusca, -ae, f.

CH. 15

WORD LIST	SINGULAR	PLURAL
i. **rādix,** rādīcis, f., *root*	rádix	rádices
ii. **truncus,** -ī, m., *trunk*	trúncus	trúnci
iii. **cacūmen,** cacūminis, n., *treetop*	cacúmen	cacúmina
iv. **rāmus,** -ī, m., *branch*	rámus	rámi
v. **rāmulus,** -ī, m., *small branch, twig*	rámulus	rámuli
vi. **folium,** -ī, n., *leaf*	fólium	fólia
vii. **frons,** frondis, f., *bough, leafy branch*	fróns	fróndes
viii. **sēmen,** sēminis, n., *seed*	sémen	sémina
ix. **cōnus,** -ī, m., *cone*	cónus	cóni
x. **nux,** nucis, -f., *nut*	núx	núces
xi. **bāca,** -ae, f., *berry (not in clusters)*	báca	bácae
xii. **acinus,** -ī, m., *berry (in clusters)*	ácinus	ácini
xiii. **cortex,** corticis, m., *bark*	córtex	córtices
xiv. **lignum,** -ī, n., *wood*	lígnum	lígna

EXTRA
liber, librī, m., *inner bark*
pōmum, -ī, n., *fruit*

lignum: materia, -ae, f.
pōmum: mālum, -ī, n.
rāmulus: sarmentum, -ī, n.; virga, -ae, f.
sēmen: grānum, -ī, n.
truncus: stīpes, stīpitis, m.; stirps, stirpis, f.

SYNONYMS
cortex: crusta, -ae f.
folium: verbēna, -ae, f.

CH. 16

WORD LIST	SINGULAR	PLURAL
i. **quercus,** -ūs, f., *oak*	quércus	quércus
ii. **rōbur,** rōboris, n., *oaken wood*	róbur	róbora
iii. **ulmus,** -ī, f., *elm*	úlmus	úlmi

WORD LIST	SINGULAR	PLURAL
iv. **pīnus,** -ī, f., *pine*	pínus	píni
v. **abiēs,** abietis, f., *fir*	ábies	abíetes
vi. **platānus,** -ī, f., *plane tree*	platánus	platáni
vii. **pōpulus,** ī, f., *poplar, cottonwood*	pópulus	pópuli
viii. **acer,** aceris, n., *maple*	ácer	ácera
ix. **salix,** salicis, f., *willow*	sálix	sálices
x. **fāgus,** -ī, f., *beech*	fágus	fági
xi. **corylus,** -ī, f., *hazel*	córylus	córyli
xii. **fraxinus,** -ī, f., *ash*	fráxinus	fráxini
xiii. **betula,** -ae, f., *birch*	bétula	bétulae
xiv. **taxus,** -ī, f., *yew*	táxus	táxi
xv. **tilia,** -ae, f., *linden tree*	tília	tíliae

EXTRA
taeda, -ae, f., *pine-pitch*

SYNONYMS
taeda: pix, picis, f.
quercus: īlex, īlicis, f.

CH. 17

WORD LIST	SINGULAR	PLURAL
i. **putāmen,** putāminis, n., *shell, peel*	putámen	putámina
ii. **cortex,** corticis, m., *husk*	córtex	córtices
iii. **nūcleus,** -ī, m., *meat of nut*	núcleus	núclei
iv. **glans,** glandis, f., *acorn*	gláns	glándes
v. **iūglans,** iūglandis, f., *walnut*	iúglans	iuglándes
vi. **castanea,** -ae, f., *chesnut*	castánea	castáneae
vii. **amygdalum,** -ī, n., *almond*	amýgdalum	amýgdala
viii. **bāca,** -ae, f., *berry (not in clusters)*	báca	bácae
ix. **olea,** -ae, f., *olive*	ólea	óleae
x. **vaccīnium,** -ī, n., *blueberry*	vaccínium	vaccínia
xi. **acinus,** -ī, m., *berry (in clusters)*	ácinus	ácini
xii. **ūva,** -ae, f., *grape*	úva	úvae
xiii. **mōrum,** -ī, n., *mulberry*	mórum	móra
xiv. **rubus,** -ī, m., *raspberry, blackberry*	rúbus	rúbi
xv. **frāgum,** -ī, n., *strawberry*	frágum	frága

EXTRA
nux, nucis, f., *nut*

SYNONYMS
olea: olīva, -ae, f.
putāmen: cortex, corticis, m.; crusta, -ae, f.

CH. 18

WORD LIST	SINGULAR	PLURAL
i. **rosa,** -ae, f., *rose*	rósa	rósae
ii. **līlium,** -ī, n., *lily*	lílium	lília
iii. **viola,** -ae, f., *violet*	víola	víolae
iv. **crocus,** -ī, m., *crocus*	crócus	cróci
v. **rānunculus,** -ī, m., *buttercup*	ranúnculus	ranúnculi
vi. **chrȳsanthemum,** -ī, n., *marigold*	chrysánthemum	chrysánthema
vii. **narcissus,** -ī, m., *narcissus, daffodil*	narcíssus	narcíssi
viii. **taraxacum,*** -ī, n., *dandelion*	taráxacum	taráxaca
ix. **myosōta,** -ae, f., *forget-me-not*	myosóta	myosótae
x. **bellis,** bellidis, f., *daisy*	béllis	béllides
xi. **hēlianthes,** hēlianthis, n., *sunflower*	heliánthes	heliántha
xii. **trifolium,** -ī, n., *clover*	trifólium	trifólia
xiii. **carduus,** -ī, m., *thistle*	cárduus	cárdui
xiv. **tulipa,*** -ae, f., *tulip*	túlipa	túlipae
xv. **hyacinthus,** -ī, m., *hyacinth*	hyacínthus	hyacínthi

EXTRA
papāver, papāveris, n., *poppy*

SYNONYMS
chrȳsanthemum: caltha, -ae, f.

CH. 19

WORD LIST	SINGULAR	PLURAL
i. **cutis,** -is, f., *skin, peel*	cútis	cútes
ii. **petiolus,** -ī, m., *fruit stem*	petíolus	petíoli
iii. **pulpa,** -ae, f., *pulp, flesh*	púlpa	púlpae
iv. **lignum,** -ī, n., *pit*	lígnum	lígna
v. **cerasum,** -ī, n., *cherry*	cérasum	cérasa
vi. **persicum,** -ī, n., *peach*	pérsicum	pérsica
vii. **prūnum,** -ī, n., *plum*	prúnum	prúna
viii. **palmula,** -ae, f., *date*	pálmula	pálmulae
ix. **volva,** -ae, f., *core, seed-wrapper*	vólva	vólvae
x. **mālum,** -ī, n., *apple*	málum	mála
xi. **pirum,** -ī, n., *pear*	pírum	píra
xii. **aurantium,*** -ī, n., *orange*	aurántium	aurántia
xiii. **cītreum,** -ī, n., *lemon, lime, citron*	cítreum	cítrea
xiv. **fīcus,** -ī, f., *fig*	fícus	fíci

WORD LIST
xv. **ariēna,** -ae, f., *banana*
xvi. **grānātum,** -ī, n., *pomegranate*

SINGULAR	PLURAL
ariéna	ariénae
granátum	granáta

SYNONYMS
grānātum: mālogrānātum, -ī, n.; mālum Pūnicum, -ī, n.

lignum: os, ossis, n.
petiolus: caulis, -is, m.

CH. 20

WORD LIST

	SINGULAR	PLURAL
i. **faba,** -ae, f., *broad bean*	fába	-----
ii. **phasēlus,** -ī, m., *kidney bean*	phasélus	-----
iii. **pīsum,** -ī, n., *pea*	písum	-----
iv. **caepa,** -ae, f., *onion*	cáepa	cáepae
v. **ālium,** -ī, n., *garlic*	álium	ália
vi. **rāpum,** -ī, n., *turnip*	rápum	rápa
vii. **raphanus,** -ī, m., *radish*	ráphanus	ráphani
viii. **pastināca,** -ae, f., *carrot, parsnip*	pastináca	pastinácae
ix. **potāta,*** -ae, f., *potato*	potáta	potátae
x. **cucurbita,** -ae, f., *squash, pumpkin*	cucúrbita	cucúrbitae
xi. **cucumis,** cucumeris, m., *cucumber*	cúcumis	cucúmeres
xii. **pepo,** peponis, m., *melon, watermelon*	pépo	pépones
xiii. **lycopersicum,*** -ī, n., *tomato*	lycopérsicum	lycopérsica
xiv. **capsicum,*** -ī, n., *hot pepper*	cápsicum	cápsica
xv. **brassica,** -ae, f., *cabbage*	brássica	brássicae
xvi. **lactūca,** -ae, f., *lettuce*	lactúca	lactúcae
xvii. **asparagus,** -ī, m., *asparagus*	aspáragus	aspáragi
xviii. **apium,** -ī, n., *parsley, celery*	ápium	ápia

EXTRA
armoracia, -ae, f., *horseradish*
blitum, -ī, n., *spinach*
cicer, ciceris, n., *chickpea, garbanzo bean*
porrum, -ī, n., *leak, scallion*

SYNONYMS
caepa: bulbus, -ī, m.
pepo: mēlopepo, mēlopepōnis, m.; mēlo, mēlōnis, m.
potāta: sōlānum,* -ī, n.

CH. 21

WORD LIST	SINGULAR	PLURAL
i. **thymum,** -ī, n., *thyme*	thýmum	-----
ii. **orīganum,** ī, n., *oregano*	oríganum	-----
iii. **rosmarīnum,** -ī, n., *rosemary*	rosmarínum	-----
iv. **ōcimum,** -ī, n., *basil*	ócimum	-----
v. **mentha,** -ae, f., *mint*	méntha	-----
vi. **laurus,** -ī, f., *laurel, bay leaf*	laúrus	laúri
vii. **cumīnum,** -ī, n., *cumin*	cumínum	-----
viii. **sināpis,** -is, f., *mustard*	sinápis	-----
ix. **piper,** -is, n., *pepper*	píper	-----
x. **anēthum,** -ī, n., *dill*	anéthum	-----
xi. **zingiber,** -is, n., *ginger*	zíngiber	-----
xii. **cinnamon,** cinnamī, n., *cinnamon*	cinnamón	-----
xiii. **saccharon,** -ī, n., *sugar, saccharin*	sáccharon	-----
xiv. **sal,** -is, f., *salt*	sál	sáles

SYNONYMS
cumīnum: cāreum, -ī, n.
rosmarīnum: ros marīnum, -ī, n.
thymum: serpyllum, -ī, n.

CH. 22

WORD LIST	SINGULAR	PLURAL
i. **corpus,** corporis, n., *body*	córpus	córpora
ii. **caput,** capitis, n., *head*	cáput	cápita
iii. **truncus,** -ī, m., *torso*	trúncus	trúnci
iv. **crūs,** crūris, n., *leg*	crús	crúra
v. **bracchium,** -ī, n., *arm*	brácchium	brácchia
vi. **pectus,** -oris, n., *chest*	péctus	péctora
vii. **alvus,** -ī, f., *belly, paunch*	álvus	álvi
viii. **umbīlicus,** -ī, m., *navel*	umbílicus	umbílici
ix. **tergum,** -ī, n., *back*	térgum	térga
x. **lumbī,** -ōrum, m. pl., *loins*	-----	lúmbi
xi. **natis,** -is, f., *buttock*	nátis	nátes
xii. **umerus,** -ī, m., *shoulder*	úmerus	úmeri
xiii. **lacertus,** -ī, m., *upper arm*	lacértus	lacérti

WORD LIST	SINGULAR	PLURAL
xiv. **cubitum,** -ī, n., *elbow*	cúbitum	cúbita
xv. **manus,** -ūs, f., *hand*	mánus	mánus
xvi. **coxa,** -ae, f., *hip*	cóxa	cóxae
xvii. **femur,** femoris, n., *thigh*	fémur	fémora
xviii. **genu,** -ūs, n., *knee*	génu	génua
xix. **tībia,** -ae, f., *shin*	tíbia	tíbiae
xx. **sūra,** -ae, f., *calf*	súra	súrae
xxi. **pēs,** pedis, m., *foot*	pés	pédes

EXTRA

anus, -ī, m., *anus*
mamma, -ae, f., *breast*
papilla, -ae, f., *nipple*
penis, -is, m., *penis*
scapula, -ae, f., *shoulder blade*
scrotum, -ī, n., *scrotum*
testis, -is, m., *testicle*
venter, ventris, m., *belly*
volva, -ae, f., *vagina*

SYNONYMS

bracchium: armus, -ī, m.
cubitum: ulna, -ae, f.
natis: clunis, -is, f.
penis: membrum virile, -is, n.
tergum: dorsum, -ī, n.

CH. 23

WORD LIST	SINGULAR	PLURAL
i. **capillus,** -ī, m., *hair (on the head)*	capíllus	capílli
ii. **auris,** -is, f., *ear*	aúris	aúres
iii. **collum,** -ī, n., *neck*	cóllum	cólla
iv. **cervix,** cervīcis, f., *nape*	cérvix	cervíces
v. **iugulum,** -ī, n., *throat, Adam's apple*	iúgulum	iúgula
vi. **facies,** -ēi, f., *face*	fácies	fácies
vii. **frons,** frontis, f., *forehead*	fróns	fróntes
viii. **tempus,** temporis, n., *temple*	témpus	témpora
ix. **oculus,** -ī, m., *eye*	óculus	óculi
x. **palpebra,** -ae, f., *eyelid; eyelash*	pálpebra	pálpebrae
xi. **supercilium,** -ī, n., *eyebrow*	supercílium	supercília
xii. **pūpilla,** -ae, f., *pupil*	pupílla	pupíllae
xiii. **gena,** -ae, f., *cheek; lower eyelid*	géna	génae
xiv. **nāsus,** -ī, m., *nose*	násus	nási
xv. **nāris,** -is, f., *nostril*	náris	náres
xvi. **ōs,** ōris, n., *mouth*	ós	óra

WORD LIST	SINGULAR	PLURAL
xvii. **lābrum,** -ī, n., *lip*	lábrum	lábra
xviii. **dens,** dentis, m., *tooth*	déns	déntes
xix. **lingua,** -ae, f., *tongue*	língua	línguae
xx. **mentum,** -ī, n., *chin*	méntum	ménta
xxi. **barba,** -ae, f., *beard*	bárba	bárbae

EXTRA	SYNONYMS
dens cavus, -ī, m., *cavity*	**capillus:** crīnis, -is, m.; capillitium, -ī, m.; coma, -ae, f.
gingiva, -ae, f., *gum*	**facies:** vultus, -ūs, m.
mucus, -ī, m., *phlegm, snot*	**gena:** bucca, -ae, f.; māla, -ae, f.
saliva, -ae, f., *saliva*	**iugulum:** guttur, -is, n.; gula, -ae, f.
uvula, -ae, f., *uvula*	**labrum:** labium, -ī, n.
	pūpilla: cora, -ae, f.; pūpula, -ae, f.
	saliva: sputum, -ī, n.

CH. 24

WORD LIST	SINGULAR	PLURAL
i. **carpus,*** -ī, m., *wrist*	cárpus	cárpi
ii. **digitus,** -ī, m., *finger*	dígitus	dígiti
iii. **pollex,** pollicis, m., *thumb*	póllex	póllices
iv. **index,** indicis, m., *pointer finger*	índex	índices
v. **medius digitus,** -ī, m., *middle finger*	médius dígitus	médii dígiti
vi. **ānulārius digitus,** -ī, m., *ring finger*	anulárius dígitus	anulárii dígiti
vii. **minimus digitus,** -ī, m., *pinky, little finger*	mínimus dígitus	mínimi dígiti
viii. **articulus,** -ī, m., *knuckle*	artículus	artículi
ix. **unguis,** -is, f., *fingernail*	únguis	úngues
x. **palma,** -ae, f., *palm*	pálma	pálmae
xi. **pugnus,** -ī, m., *fist*	púgnus	púgni
xii. **tālus,** -ī, m., *ankle*	tálus	táli
xiii. **calx,** calcis, f., *heel*	cálx	cálces
xiv. **planta,** -ae, f., *sole*	plánta	plántae
xv. **digitus (pedis),** -ī, m., *toe*	dígitus pédis	dígiti pédis/pédu
xvi. **allus,** -ī, m., *big toe*	állus	álli

EXTRA
cutīcula, -ae, f., *cuticle*
ruga, -ae, f., *wrinkle*

SYNONYMS
anularius: quartus digitus, -ī, m.
calx: calcaneum, -ī, n.
carpus: prima palmae pars, partis, f.

CH. 25

WORD LIST	SINGULAR	PLURAL
i. **cerebrum,** -ī, n., *brain*	cérebrum	cérebra
ii. **trăchīa,** -ae, f., *trachia*	trachía	trachíae
iii. **pulmo,** pulmōnis, m., *lung*	púlmo	pulmónes
iv. **cor,** cordis, n., *heart*	cór	córda
v. **sanguis,** sanguinis, m., *blood*	sánguis	-----
vi. **artēria,** -ae, f., *artery*	artéria	artériae
vii. **rēnēs,** rēnum, m. pl., *kidneys*	-----	rénes
viii. **vēna,** -ae, f., *vein*	véna	vénae
ix. **faucēs,** faucium, f. pl., *throat*	-----	faúces
x. **venter,** ventris, m., *stomach*	vénter	véntres
xi. **viscera,** -um, n. pl., *organs, innards*	-----	víscera
xii. **iecur,** iecoris, n., *liver*	iécur	iécora
xiii. **fel,** fellis, n., *gall bladder, bile*	fél	-----
xiv. **vēsīca,** -ae, f., *bladder*	vēsīca	-----
xv. **cōlon,** -ī, n., *colon*	cólon	cóla

EXTRA
musculus, -ī, m., *muscle*
nervus, -ī, m., *sinew*
stercus, stercoris, n., *dung, excrement*
ūrīna, -ae, f., *urine*
uterus, -ī, m., *womb*

SYNONYMS
faucēs: gula, -ae, f.; guttur, -is, n.
fel: bīlis, -is, f.
ūrīna: lotium, -ī, n.
venter: stomachus, -ī, m.
viscera: exta, -ōrum, n. pl.; intestīna, -ōrum, n. pl.

CH. 26

WORD LIST	SINGULAR	PLURAL
i. **os,** ossis, n., *bone*	ós	óssa
ii. **artus,** -ūs, m., *joint*	ártus	ártus
iii. **medulla,** -ae, f., *marrow*	medúlla	-----
iv. **calvāria,** -ae, f., *skull*	calvária	calváriae
v. **maxilla,** -ae, f., *jaw*	maxílla	maxíllae
vi. **spīna,** -ae, f., *backbone*	spína	spínae
vii. **vertebra,** -ae, f., *vertebra*	vertébra	vertébrae
viii. **costa,** -ae, f., *rib*	cósta	cóstae
ix. **umerus,** -ī, m., *umerus*	úmerus	úmeri
x. **radius,** -ī, m., *radius*	rádius	rádii
xi. **ulna,** -ae, f., *ulna*	úlna	úlnae
xii. **coxa,** -ae, f., *coxa*	cóxa	cóxae
xiii. **femur,** femoris, n., *thigh bone*	fémur	fémora
xiv. **patella,** -ae, f., *patella, knee cap*	patélla	patéllae
xv. **tībia,** -ae, f., *tibia, shin bone*	tíbia	tíbiae
xvi. **fībula,** -ae, f., *fibula, ankle bone*	fíbula	fíbulae

EXTRA

malleolus,* -ī, m., *ankle bone*

SYNONYMS

maxilla: māla, -ae, f.

CH. 27

WORD LIST	SINGULAR	PLURAL
i. **mons,** montis, m., *mountain*	móns	móntes
ii. **culmen,** culminis, n., *peak, top*	cúlmen	cúlmina
iii. **rūpes,** rupis, f., *cliff*	rúpes	rúpes
iv. **iugum,** -ī, n., *mountain ridge*	iúgum	iúga
v. **collis,** -is, m., *hill*	cóllis	cólles
vi. **vallis,** -is, f., *valley*	vállis	válles
vii. **convallis,** -is, f., *ravine*	convállis	conválles
viii. **plānities,** -ēī, f., *plain*	planíties	planíties
ix. **fons,** fontis, m., *spring, fountain*	fóns	fóntes
x. **rīvus,** -ī, m., *stream, creek*	rívus	rívi
xi. **flūmen,** flūminis, n., *river*	flúmen	flúmina
xii. **rīpa,** -ae, f., *bank*	rípa	rípae
xiii. **mare,** -is, n., *sea*	máre	mária

WORD LIST	SINGULAR	PLURAL
xiv. **ōs,** ōris, n., *mouth (of a river)*	ós	óra
xv. **cataracta,** -ae, f., *waterfall*	catarácta	cataráctae
xvi. **stagnum,** -ī, n., *pond*	stágnum	stágna
xvii. **palus,** palūdis, f., *swamp, marsh*	pálus	páludes

EXTRA
lacūna, -ae, f., *pool*
lacus, -ūs, m., *lake*

SYNONYMS
collis: tumulus, -ī, m.
culmen: cacūmen, cacūminis, n.

flūmen: amnis, -is, m.; fluvius, -ī, m.
mare: aequor, -is, n.; pelagus, -ī, n.; pontus, -ī, m.
ōs: ōstium, -ī, n.
plānities: plāna, -ae, f.
rīpa: lītus, lītoris, n. [of the sea]
rūpes: scopulus, -ī, m.

CH. 28

WORD LIST	SINGULAR	PLURAL
i. **lītus,** lītoris, n., *sea shore, coastline*	lítus	lítora
ii. **prōmonturium,** -ī, n., *headland*	promontúrium	promontúria
iii. **sinus,** -ūs, m., *bay, gulf, inlet*	sínus	sínus
iv. **fluctus,** -ūs, m., *wave*	fluctus	fluctūs
v. **spūma,** -ae, f., *foam*	spúma	spúmae
vi. **aestus,** -ūs, m., *tide*	aéstus	aéstus
vii. **vorāgo,** vorāginis, f., *whirlpool*	vorágo	worágines
viii. **aequor,** -is, n., *flat sea, calm sea*	aéquor	aéquora
ix. **altum,** -ī, n., *the deep, high sea*	áltum	álta
x. **vadum,** -ī, n., *the shallows, shoals*	vádum	váda
xi. **scopulus,** -ī, m., *rock (jutting from sea)*	scópulus	scópuli
xii. **fretum,** -ī, n., *strait*	frétum	fréta
xiii. **isthmus,** -ī, m., *isthmus*	ísthmus	ísthmi
xiv. **insula,** -ae, f., *island*	ínsula	ínsulae
xv. **paenīnsula,** -ae, f., *peninsula*	paenínsula	paenínsulae

SYNONYMS
fluctus: unda, -ae, f.
lītus: ōra maritima, -ae, f.
vorāgo: vertex, verticis, m.; gurges, gurgitis, m.

CH. 29

WORD LIST	SINGULAR	PLURAL
i. **sōl,** sōlis, m., *sun*	sól	sóles
ii. **caelum,** -ī, n., *sky*	caélum	caéli[1]
iii. **dies,** -ēī, m./f., *day*	díes	díes
iv. **aurōra,** -ae, f., *dawn*	auróra	aurórae
v. **crepusculum,** -ī, n., *twilight*	crepúsculum	crepúscula
vi. **īris,** īridis, f., *rainbow*	íris	írides
vii. **nox,** noctis, f., *night*	nóx	nóctes
viii. **lūna,** -ae, f., *moon*	lúna	lúnae
ix. **stella,** -ae, f., *star*	stélla	stéllae
x. **constellātio,** constellātiōnis, f., *constellation*	constellátio	constellatiónes
xi. **planēta,** -ae, f., *planet*	planéta	planétae
xii. **comētēs,** -ae, f., *comet*	cométes	cométae
xiii. **eclīpsis,** -is, f., *eclipse*	eclípsis	eclípses
xiv. **noctua,** -ae, f., *owl, night bird*	nóctua	nóctuae
xv. **vespertīlio,** vespertīliōnis, f., *bat*	vespertílio	vespertiliónes

EXTRA
fax, facis, f. (caelestis), *meteor, shooting star*
vesper, -is, f., *evening*

SYNONYMS
aurōra: dīlūculum, -ī, n.
caelum: dīvum, -ī, n.
constellātio: sīdus, sīderis, n.
īris: arcus pluvialis, -is, m.
stella: aster, -is, m.; sīdus, sīderis, n.

CH. 30

WORD LIST	SINGULAR	PLURAL
i. **nūbes,** -is, f., *cloud*	núbes	núbes
ii. **cālīgo,** cālīginis, f., *fog*	calígo	calígines
iii. **nimbus,** -ī, m., *raincloud*	nímbus	nímbi
iv. **imber,** imbris, m., *rain*	ímber	ímbres
v. **nix,** nivis, f., *snow*	níx	níves

---

1. The plural of *caelum* is usually masculine.

WORD LIST	SINGULAR	PLURAL
vi. **grando,** grandinis, f., *hail*	grándo	grándines
vii. **tempestās,** tempestātis, f., *storm*	tempéstas	tempestátes
viii. **fulgur,** -is, n., *lightning*	fúlgur	fúlgura
ix. **fulmen,** fulminis, n., *lightning bolt*	fúlmen	fúlmina
x. **tonitrus,** -ūs, m., *thunder*	tónitrus	tónitrus
xi. **dīluvium,** -ī, n., *flood*	dilúvium	dilúvia
xii. **aura,** -ae, f., *breeze*	aúra	aúrae
xiii. **procella,** -ae, f., *gale*	procélla	procéllae
xiv. **turbo,** turbinis, m., *whirlwind, tornado*	túrbo	túrbines

EXTRA
calor, calōris, m., *heat*
frīgus, frīgoris, n., *cold*
glacies, -ēī, f., *ice*
styria, -ae, f., *icicle*
terrae lapsus, -ūs, m., *earthquake*
ventus, -ī, m., *wind*

SYNONYMS
aura: flāmen, flāminis, m.
cālīgo: nebula, -ae, f.
imber: pluvia, -ae, f.

CH. 31

WORD LIST	SINGULAR	PLURAL
i. **glaeba,** -ae, f., *clod*	gláeba	gláebae
ii. **caespes,** caespitis, m., *turf*	caéspes	caéspites
iii. **saxum,** -ī, n., *rock*	sáxum	sáxa
iv. **lapis,** lapidis, m., *stone*	lápis	lápides
v. **sabulo,** sabulōnis, m., *gravel*	sábulo	-----
vi. **līmus,** -ī, m., *mud*	límus	-----
vii. **silva,** -ae, f., *forest*	sílva	sílvae
viii. **lūcus,** -ī, m., *grove, stand*	lúcus	lúci
ix. **campus,** -ī, m., *field*	cámpus	cámpi
x. **prātum,** -ī, n., *meadow*	prátum	práta
xi. **antrum,** -ī, n., *cave*	ántrum	ántra
xii. **sōlitūdo,** sōlitūdinis, f., *wilderness, wasteland*	solitúdo	solitúdines
xiii. **harēnae,** -ārum, f. pl., *desert*	-----	harénae
xiv. **palus,** palūdis, f., *swamp, marsh*	pálus	palúdes
xv. **rūpes,** -is, f., *cliff*	rúpes	rúpes

EXTRA
calculus, -ī, m., *pebble*
saltus, -ūs, m., *mixed forests, meadows, and hills*

SYNONYMS
antrum: caverna, -ae, f.; specus, -ūs, m.; spelunca, -ae, f.
līmus: caenum, -ī, n.; lutum, -ī, n.
silva: nemus, nemoris, n.
sabulo: glārea, -ae, f.
palus: stagnum, -ī, n.

CH. 32

WORD LIST	SINGULAR	PLURAL
i. **spīca,** -ae, f., *head, ear*	spíca	spícae
ii. **grānum,** -ī, n., *grain, kernel*	gránum	grána
iii. **furfur,** -is, m., *bran*	fúrfur	fúrfures
iv. **glūma,** -ae, f., *hull, husk*	glúma	glúmae
v. **palea,** -ae, f., *chaff*	pálea	páleae
vi. **arista,** -ae, f., *beard (of wheat), awn*	arísta	arístae
vii. **flōs,** flōris, m., *flower*	flós	flóres
viii. **gemma,** -ae, f., *bud*	gémma	gémmae
ix. **caulis,** -is, f., *stem*	caúlis	caúles
x. **calyx,** calycis, m., *calyx, sepals*	cályx	cályces
xi. **petalium,*** -ī, n., *petal*	petálium	petália
xii. **corolla,*** -ae, f., *corolla*	corólla	coróllae
xiii. **pistillum,*** -ī, n., *pistil*	pistíllum	pistílla
xiv. **stigma,*** stigmatis, n., *stigma*	stígma	stígmata
xv. **stāmen,*** stāminis, n., *stamen*	stámen	stámina
xvi. **anthēra,*** -ae, f., *anthera*	anthéra	anthérae
xvii. **pollen,*** pollinis, n., *pollen*	póllen	-------

EXTRA
herba, -ae, f., *blade of grass*

SYNONYMS
anthēra: fīlum, -ī, n.
petalium: folium (floris), -ī, n.
pollen: farina, -ae, f.

APPENDIX OF DECLENSIONS

Pure Latin Declensions

-a, -ae, f./m.
(1st Fem./Masc.)

	singular	plural
nominative	besti-a	besti-ae
accusative	besti-am	besti-ās
genitive	besti-ae	besti-ārum
dative	besti-ae	besti-īs
ablative	besti-ā	besti-īs

-us, -ī, m./f.
(2nd Masc./Fem.)

	singular	plural
nominative	pull-us	pull-ī
accusative	pull-um	pull-ōs
genitive	pull-ī	pull-ōrum
dative	pull-ō	pull-īs
ablative	pull-ō	pull-īs

-um, -ī, n.
(2nd Neut.)

	singular	plural
nominative	ōv-um	ōv-a
accusative	ōv-um	ōv-a
genitive	ōv-ī	ōv-ōrum
dative	ōv-ō	ōv-īs
ablative	ōv-ō	ōv-īs

—, *-is*, m./f.
(3rd Masc./Fem. w/ stem change)

	singular	plural
nominative	pēs	ped-ēs
accusative	ped-em	ped-ēs
genitive	ped-is	ped-um
dative	ped-ī	ped-ibus
ablative	ped-e	ped-ibus

-is, -is, m./f.
(3rd Masc./Fem. w/o stem change)

	singular	plural
nominative	av-is	av-ēs
accusative	av-em	av-ēs
genitive	av-is	av-ium
dative	av-ī	av-ibus
ablative	av-e	av-ibus

—, *-is*, n.
(3rd Neut. w/ stem change)

	singular	plural
nominative	pectus	pector-a
accusative	pectus	pector-a
genitive	pector-is	pector-um
dative	pector-ī	pector-ibus
ablative	pector-e	pector-ibus

-ar/are/al/ale, -is, n.
(3rd Neut. w/o stem change)

	singular	plural
nominative	animal	animāl-ia
accusative	animal	animāl-ia
genitive	animāl-is	animāl-ium
dative	animāl-ī	animāl-ibus
ablative	animāl-ī	animāl-ibus

-us, -ūs, m./f.
(4th Masc./Fem.)

	singular	plural
nominative	man-us	man-ūs
accusative	man-um	man-ūs
genitive	man-ūs	man-uum
dative	man-uī	man-ibus
ablative	man-ū	man-ibus

-u, -ūs, n.
(4th Neut.)

	singular	plural
nominative	gen-u	gen-ua
accusative	gen-u	gen-ua
genitive	gen-ūs	gen-uum
dative	gen-uī	gen-ibus
ablative	gen-ū	gen-ibus

-es, ēī, f./m.
(5th Masc./Fem.)

	singular	plural
nominative	di-es	di-ēs
accusative	di-em	di-ēs
genitive	di-ēī	di-ērum
dative	di-ēī	di-ēbus
ablative	di-ē	di-ēbus

Greek Declensions in Latin

-ē, -ēs, f.
(Greek 1st Fem.)

	singular	plural
nominative	alk-ē	alk-ae
accusative	alk-ēn	alk-ās
genitive	alk-ēs	alk-ārum
dative	alk-ae	alk-īs
ablative	alk-ē/ā	alk-īs

-os, -ī, m.
(Greek 2nd Masc.)

	singular	plural
nominative	haliaet-os	haliaet-ī
accusative	haliaet-on	haliaet-ōs
genitive	haliaet-ī	haliaet-ōrum
dative	haliaet-ō	haliaet-īs
ablative	haliaet-ō	haliaet-īs

-on, -ī, n.
(Greek 2nd Neut.)

	singular	plural
nominative	saccar-on	saccar-a
accusative	saccar-on	saccar-a
genitive	saccar-ī	saccar-ōrum
dative	saccar-ō	saccar-īs
ablative	saccar-ō	saccar-īs

—, *-is*, m./f.
(Greek 3rd Masc./Fem.)

	singular	plural
nominative	procyōn	procyōn-ēs
accusative	procyōn-a	procyōn-ēs
genitive	procyōn-is	procyōn-um
dative	procyōn-ī	procyōn-ibus
ablative	procyōn-e	procyōn-ibus

-ma, -matis, n.
(Greek 3rd Neut.)

	singular	plural
nominative	stigm-a	stigmat-a
accusative	stigm-a	stigmat-a
genitive	stigmat-is	stigmat-um
dative	stigmat-ī	stigmat-īs
ablative	stigmat-e	stigmat-īs

CPSIA information can be obtained
at www.ICGtesting.com
Printed in the USA
FSOW03n0338120515
6995FS